CAMBRIDGE LIBRARY COLLECTION

Books of enduring scholarly value

History

The books reissued in this series include accounts of historical events and movements by eye-witnesses and contemporaries, as well as landmark studies that assembled significant source materials or developed new historiographical methods. The series includes work in social, political and military history on a wide range of periods and regions, giving modern scholars ready access to influential publications of the past.

The Cambridge Modern History

At the time of its conception in 1896, the *Cambridge Modern History* was envisaged as a 'great English universal history'. Six years later, the first volume was published, and reprinted within a month. The project would take years to complete, and just before the publication of the tenth volume in 1907, this short work was published by Cambridge University Press in order to promote the volumes and the project's history. The book opens with the origin of the project and the early plans of Lord Acton, its first editor. Also included are ten extracts from various volumes, along with the names of the first contributors, who delivered their chapters from as far afield as America, Germany, and Italy. Later chapters offer a short history of Cambridge University Press, an account of the production techniques used, and the terms by which the books (and their specially designed bookstand) could be obtained.

Cambridge University Press has long been a pioneer in the reissuing of out-of-print titles from its own backlist, producing digital reprints of books that are still sought after by scholars and students but could not be reprinted economically using traditional technology. The Cambridge Library Collection extends this activity to a wider range of books which are still of importance to researchers and professionals, either for the source material they contain, or as landmarks in the history of their academic discipline.

Drawing from the world-renowned collections in the Cambridge University Library, and guided by the advice of experts in each subject area, Cambridge University Press is using state-of-the-art scanning machines in its own Printing House to capture the content of each book selected for inclusion. The files are processed to give a consistently clear, crisp image, and the books finished to the high quality standard for which the Press is recognised around the world. The latest print-on-demand technology ensures that the books will remain available indefinitely, and that orders for single or multiple copies can quickly be supplied.

The Cambridge Library Collection will bring back to life books of enduring scholarly value (including out-of-copyright works originally issued by other publishers) across a wide range of disciplines in the humanities and social sciences and in science and technology.

The Cambridge Modern History

An Account of Its Origin, Authorship and Production

Anonymous

CAMBRIDGE UNIVERSITY PRESS

Cambridge, New York, Melbourne, Madrid, Cape Town,
Singapore, São Paolo, Delhi, Tokyo, Mexico City

Published in the United States of America by Cambridge University Press, New York

www.cambridge.org
Information on this title: www.cambridge.org/9781108036696

This edition first published 1907
This digitally printed version 2011

ISBN 978-1-108-03669-6 Paperback

THE

CAMBRIDGE

MODERN HISTORY

THE
CAMBRIDGE
MODERN HISTORY

AN ACCOUNT OF ITS
ORIGIN, AUTHORSHIP AND PRODUCTION

Cambridge
at the University Press
1907

𝕮ambridge :
PRINTED BY JOHN CLAY, M.A.
AT THE UNIVERSITY PRESS.

CONTENTS

JOHN EMERICH EDWARD, first LORD ACTON

Photograph by Elliott and Fry

THE CAMBRIDGE MODERN HISTORY

CHAPTER I.

LORD ACTON AND THE PLANNING OF THE HISTORY

N February 1896, Lord Acton held the Regius Professorship of Modern History at Cambridge. A year had past since he had settled, 'in a happier hour' as he spoke of it himself, in the University which, five-and-forty years before, he had hoped to join. His devotion to truth, his ideal of perfection, his learning and his cosmopolitan outlook were already impressed on historical studies and on Cambridge.

The influence which Lord Acton exercised, both at Cambridge and elsewhere, can readily be understood. To quote a writer in *The Athenæum* 'No glorified encyclopædia, no aggregate of unrelated facts confronted the inquirer who interrogated Lord Acton, but a soul in whom spoke, as it seemed, the wisdom of the ages, and from whose depths there issued the very oracles of history, shining with the light that comes of absolutely single love of truth, penetrating even the gloom of the future by an illuminative knowledge of the past......To be with Acton was like being with the cultivated mind of Europe incarnate in its finest characteristics. In the deep tones of his voice there seemed to sound the accents of history. In those unflinching phrases we heard the impersonal estimate of the future, weighing in unerring balance the thoughts and deeds of the actors of the present or past, with a knowledge that knew no gap.'

So when, early in the year 1896, the idea of a great English Universal History came to the Syndics of the Cambridge Press, and they turned to Lord Acton, it was not solely by virtue of his Chair. For, position apart, there could have been no better help than his in the planning of *The Cambridge Modern History*.

How Lord Acton received the suggestion made to him, appears from a letter he addressed in March 1896 to the Secretary to the Syndics of the Press :—

'The suggestion conveyed in your letter, on the part of the Syndics, would be felt as an honour by any man, and is especially grateful to me, as cementing my recent connection with the University, and crowning its generous reception of an intruder.

'Regarding it as a first, preliminary step, I beg leave to say that I am ready provisionally, and to the same degree as a First Reading, to entertain the idea, and to give it my best consideration, until the time comes when the scheme has ripened, and you require a definite and final answer, on a fuller survey of all the conditions.

'The idea you deposited in my mind, when you spoke to me last month, was this : whether a Syndicate, utilising the best resources of such an intellectual centre as Cambridge, might not advantageously undertake to do, for the next generation, what Weber attempted for the last.... Two things appear to me certain, on the threshold : there is no man who can do it, and no work that can serve as a basis for translation or adaptation.

'After that, a number of problems arise. Do you think of a serious compilation, or of an original work? The first might be managed by a fair division of labour in Cambridge itself, or nearly. The other would require you to employ all the best men that can be got to work, in England, and I should hope some in America.'

This preliminary point having been determined, by the decision to produce an original work and no mere compilation, Lord Acton received a definite request to undertake the editorship, and accepted it in these terms :—

'I must ask leave to express my thanks to the Syndicate of the Press for their invitation to join in so important an undertaking. I have not hesitated as much as I ought to do, on account of the difficulty, because my office here makes it a duty not to be declined, and because such an opportunity of promoting his own ideas for the treatment of history has seldom been given to any man.'

This letter was dated 21 May 1896, and, soon afterwards, it was arranged that Lord Acton should prepare a full and detailed report on the scheme. This report, which was laid before the Syndics in the following October, is of great interest, both as an expression of Lord Acton's ideas and as an indication of the lines on which, in the main, *The Cambridge Modern History* has proceeded. Before giving extracts from the report, which has never before been published, it will be of interest to print part of another letter addressed by Lord Acton to the Secretary to the Syndics. It is dated 15 July 1896, and was written while Lord Acton was at work on the report :—

'There is one matter on which I desire to secure your agreement, in view of the time when I shall bring it before the Syndicate. I mean to say, that universal history is not the sum of all particular histories, and ought to be contemplated, first, in its distinctive essence, as Renaissance, Reformation, Religious Wars, Absolute Monarchy, Revolution, etc. The several countries may or may not contribute to feed the main stream, and the distribution of matter must be made accordingly. The history of nations that are off the line must not suffer ; it must be told as accurately as if the whole was divided into annals. But attention ought not to be dispersed, by putting Portugal, Transylvania, Iceland, side by side with

France and Germany. I wish to speak of them when they are important, and not whether or no, according to date. They are important and intelligible in their own sequence, and should be told in that way, not broken into bits, according to chronological order. I would have no Russian chapter until Russia becomes a factor in general history, under Peter the Great. His reign would be introduced by a sufficient and connected retrospect of intransitive Muscovy. So with Sweden, Prussia and others. When Venice, after a last appearance, early in the seventeenth century, vanishes from the scene, and lives for herself, there should be a prospective sketch, down to 1797.

'In this way, every part would have a meaning, and local history would possess unity, even if it does not point outwards, or serve any cause but its own. What is successive is connected by the law of causation; what is simultaneous is not connected by any law or any cause but accident. The objection is that so much and such energetic grouping, in obedience to ideas and not to dates, is difficult to carry out, and to explain to unwilling writers......I venture to think that it can be done, and will add considerably to the philosophic unity, the significance, and the interest of what will be a history but not a chronicle.'

Then, in October, came the detailed report to the Syndics, from which the following is an extract :—

'I submit the following observations in reply to the question proposed by the Syndics.

'The idea of a Universal Modern History has been executed with success already, both in France and in Germany. I do not allude to Oncken or to Weiss, for Oncken's 24 volumes form a series of independent works, without any attempt to fuse the materials together, and Weiss addresses an exclusive public. Our competing predecessors would be Weber of Heidelberg, and the authors of the general history which appears under the direction of Lavisse and Rambaud. Both of these have mastered the difficulties of the task which is before us.

'Weber comes in about 4000 pages from the XVth Century to the Revolution, and to the present day in as many more. The Frenchmen, who have got down to 1800, observe nearly the same proportion. Therefore, twelve volumes, each with 650 pages of text, and 550 words to a page, would have a slight advantage, in quantity, over the only rivals that occupy the ground.

'Weber's *Weltgeschichte*, lately revised by his friends, is a useful compilation; and the *Histoire Générale*, written almost entirely by experts, is a superlative work of reference. The University of Cambridge, with its resources and prestige, is in a position to aim higher, and to accomplish more.

'I propose to divide the history of the last 400 years into short chapters, averaging 30 pages, each complete in itself, and dealing with one topic, or a single group of events, accurately defined. And I would distribute them among the largest number of available writers, inviting every English historian who is competent, to contribute at least a chapter.

'It would be history not as it appears to the generality of instructed men, and is taught all the world over, but as each of the several parts is known to the man who knows it best. There would be a clean text, without foot-notes, or foreign quotations, or reference to particular authorities. The name of the author would be the reader's security for obtaining, without discussion or parade, the most perfect narrative that any English or American scholar can supply, in the appointed space.

'It will be necessary to prescribe exact limits and conditions, and to explain clearly what we desire to obtain, and to avoid. We shall avoid the needless utterance of opinion, and the service of a cause. Contributors will understand that we are established, not under the meridian of Greenwich, but in longitude 30 West; that our Waterloo must be one that satisfies French and English, Germans and Dutch alike; that nobody can tell, without examining the list of authors, where the Bishop of Oxford laid down the pen, and whether Fairbairn or Gasquet, Liebermann or Harrison, took it up.

'It is a unique opportunity of recording, in the way most useful to the greatest number, the fulness of the knowledge which the nineteenth century is about to bequeath. A mere reproduction of accepted facts would fall below the occasion, and behind the memorable date.

'In some instances, where there is nothing new to tell, we shall adopt the words of Thiers: "on est déjà bien assez nouveau par cela seul qu'on est vrai." Nobody, with 30 pages to do it in, can aspire to improve on Pastor's *Popes of the Renaissance*, Ritter's *Counter Reformation*, Holst's *Constitutional History of Slavery*, Treitschke's *Germany during the Peace*, or Brückner's and Vandal's volumes on Russia. Where all accessible information has been thoroughly absorbed, where the work is new and, for the moment, final, intelligent boiling down will be sometimes enough for our purpose. But we shall not often be left to this resource, and I hope that almost every page will be a light to every reader. We must raise the whole to the level of our best men, and discourage second-hand studies.

'It used to be meritorious to compose history, as Hallam did, without any original matter beyond the usual authorities. Raumer, at the height of his credit, renounced the easy quest of the unknown, and based his Modern History on the assumption that all requisite knowledge may be had from common books. The new material in Ranke's *Reformation* appeared so scanty as to create an impression that there was nothing more to discover, and Lingard was glad that Macaulay's narrative compelled but few changes in his own. Macaulay would hardly apply Lingard's words to himself, if he could see what his successors have made of the subject on which he satisfied the demand of his contemporaries; and Ranke's book seems to us divided by more than half a century from the Reformation as it is known to Kawerau.

'There has been not only progress but subversion and renewal since manuscripts have come into use almost without limit; since crowds of scholars are on the watch for them, and the supply of documents exceeds the supply of histories. The policy of concealment, abandoned in so many places, as neither Italy nor Prussia was interested in keeping the secrets of fallen governments whose records were in their hands, has broken down altogether, and at last the Vatican discloses the guarded treasures of Galileo's tower.

'The printing of archives has gone on parallel with the admission of enquirers, and the Master of the Rolls alone has made public 500 volumes of sources. Other countries are as profuse. While the Camden Club has produced 75 volumes, one Spanish Collection, the Documentos Ineditos, extends to half as many more. The Historical MSS. Commission is proud of its 46 volumes; but a single Russian family, the Woronsows, have issued about as many from their own family papers. At Vienna there is one series in 48 volumes, another in 83, and a third in 126; at Berlin, one in 65, and a much larger one at Florence.

'The example is followed in every province of Italy, France and Germany. Even Croatia has reached the 28th volume of its records. The Venetian despatches from Austria, those of the Nuncios from Germany, those from all parts regarding critical stages in Bavarian history, are being methodically edited. At Rome, in 1857, Doellinger drew up a remonstrance against the suppression of the Acta Tridentina, and urged that there were no means of deciding between Pallavicini and Father Paul. The Council of Trent is known to us now, not through those rivals, but from the evidence that was before them, and from much besides. Between 200 and 300 of Calvin's letters were known when Dyer wrote his Life: ten times as many are in print to-day. Above 20 volumes of Frederic's correspondence have appeared since Carlyle.

'The entire bulk of new matter which the last 40 years have supplied amounts to many thousands of volumes. The honest student finds himself continually deserted, retarded, misled by the classics of historical literature, and has to hew his own way through multitudinous transactions, periodicals and official publications, where it is difficult to sweep the horizon or to keep abreast. By the judicious division of labour, we should be able to do it, and to bring home to every man the last document, and the ripest conclusions of international research.

'Ultimate history we cannot have in this generation; but we can dispose of conventional history, and show the point we have reached on the road from the one to the other, now that all information is within reach, and every problem has become capable of solution.

'All this does not apply to our own time, and the last volumes will be concerned with secrets that cannot be learned from books, but from men. Although so much has been done for Cavour and Bismarck, we have little authentic literature about Napoleon III, and less about Thiers. After Sir Theodore Martin, Windsor is silent; Lord Rowton conceals one part of our story; Spencer Walpole has left half told another; and much more is buried in a tower at Hawarden.

'If we employ the right men, and establish a claim to confidence, we may hope to give a good account even of the Victorian era. Certain privately printed memoirs, such as Lord Broughton's, may not be absolutely inaccessible; the papers of one Prime Minister are in type, and part is in my custody; and there are elderly men about town, gorged with esoteric knowledge. For the unwritten history of later times, as for the unprinted history of earlier times, all will depend on the successful selection of writers.

'A true scholar, who is asked to contribute to a monumental work a couple of sheets on the one subject that most occupies his thoughts, and who has several years allowed him for the purpose, can hardly plead want of time.......I have a hypothetical list of about 120 men whom I should be glad to secure. At close quarters, some will turn out to be men in buckram; but, when we have consulted the best advice about contributors, at Oxford, in the North, in Ireland and America, at the Museum and the Rolls, at the Public Offices, for India, the Colonies, and War, among the clergy, the lawyers and the Jews, we shall have as many new suggestions as there will be names to expunge, and we shall still have before us a conjectural 120. Assuming that one half are sure to decline or to fail us, I would undertake the task, as I conceive it, with the remainder.......

'*The Cambridge Modern History* ought to be the composition of English, American and Colonial pens. But in an emergency, we must take a capable foreigner rather than an inferior countryman.......Every part of the work must be planed down and made flush, and we shall be obliged to negotiate a good deal, touching the rightful books to employ and the matters which the economy of the whole work requires to be included under each particular head.

'If we treat history as a progressive science, and lean specially on that side of it, the question will arise how we justify our departure from ancient ways, and how we satisfy the world that there is reason and method in our innovations. If our Wallenstein is very unlike Ranke's; if our Burke is neither the Burke of Morley, nor of Lecky; if we differ both from Taine and Sorel in the Revolution, our verba magistri will not avail against greater masters.

'To meet this difficulty we must provide a copious, accurate and well digested catalogue of authorities. Lavisse and Rambaud have done it most successfully. They devote 30 or 40 pages to their Bibliography, and give at least 1500 titles, in each volume. Even with less space, and a severer choice, we might make this feature a most valuable aid to historical studies. Our principle would be to supply help to students, not material to historians. But in critical places we must indicate minutely the sources we follow, and must refer not only to the important books, but to articles in periodical works, and even to original documents, and to transcripts in libraries.

'The result would amount to an ordinary volume, presenting a conspectus of historical literature and enumerating all the better books, the newly acquired sources and the last discoveries. It would exhibit in the clearest light the vast difference between history, original and authentic, and history, antiquated and lower than highwater mark of present learning.

'By Universal History I understand that which is distinct from the combined history of all countries, which is not a rope of sand, but a continuous development, and is not a burden on the memory, but an illumination of the soul. It moves in a succession to which the nations are subsidiary. Their story will be told, not for their own sake, but in reference and subordination to a higher series, according to the time and the degree in which they contribute to the common fortunes of mankind. Secondary states appear, in perspective, when they carry flame or fuel, not when they are isolated, irrelevant, stagnant, inarticulate, sterile, passive, when they lend nothing to the forward progress or the upward growth, and offer no aid in solving the perpetual problem of the future.

'Renaissance and the Epoch of Discovery, Reformation and Wars of Religion, Turkish Crusade and Western Colonization, European Absolutism, Dutch, English, American, French Revolution and its derivatives, the constitutional, democratic, national, Social, Liberal, Federal, movement of the world— that is the great argument of the epic that we are to expose. These things are extraterritorial, having their home in the sky, and no more confined to race or frontier than a rainbow or a storm.

'I would keep to the main line, attending to the byways at the junction only, and direct our thought on the common effort, the central action of men, by which the landmarks of civilization have been extended, and the moving force renewed. I would tell all we know of Solyman, Sixtus, Warren Hastings, not of every Sultan, Pope, or Governor General. Geneva would be prominent under Calvin, Portugal under Pombal, Corsica under Paoli; but they would otherwise retire into obscurity. Switzerland slumbers from the Reformation to the Revolution; Denmark, from 1660 to 1770; Venice, from the beginning of the seventeenth century; Holland, from the beginning of the eighteenth. We should give a retrospect of the history of Russia when it emerges, under Peter the Great, thereby following the natural order of cause, not that of fortuitous juxtaposition. I think Taine is right when he says : " Pour expliquer les événements, il suffit de les disposer dans l'ordre convenable. C'est dire leur cause que leur donner leur place."

'Whilst we give general history and not national, unless as tributary, so also we give general history, not that of religion and philosophy, of literature, science and art. They, too, appear at many points and influence the course of public events from time to time; but when they do not, then we are not concerned with them, and have not to describe their orbit when there is no conjunction.

'It may be said that these are vulgar and retrograde notions, contracting the sphere and degrading the level of history; that we might enrich it with what men have thought as well as wrought; that the true mark and measure of the age would be a work combining the method and the wisdom of Buckle and Draper, Whewell and Leslie Stephen, Burckhardt and Lamprecht, Harnack and Haym, Ihering and Gierke and Sohm. I wish I knew how all these strains could be blended ; but it is certain that we must present history in the way most widely accepted.

' I would meet the objection, and unite the moral and in-tellectual realm with that of political force, on the following plan. There would be a chapter, at intervals, on each branch of literature, when it attains supremacy, and impresses its character on the age.......This portion of the plan will be the most difficult to execute, and it is impossible, without much detail, to explain how I hope to conquer the obvious dangers, and to make it practical and scientific....I do not wish to reduce all history to a mere narrative of political transactions.

' If History is often called the teacher and the guide that regulates public life, which, to individuals as to societies, is as important as private, this is the time and the place to prove the title. The recent past contains the key to the present time. All forms of thought that influence it come before us in their turn, and we have to describe the ruling currents, to interpret the sovereign forces, that still govern and divide the world.   There are, I suppose, at least a score of them, in politics, economics, philosophy and religion, and our treatment cannot be complete, or systematic, or made to scale.

'But if we carry history down to the last syllable of recorded time, and leave the reader at the point where study passes into action, we must explain to him the cause, and the growth, and the power of every great intellectual movement, and equip him for many encounters of life.   The part thus assigned to our later volumes is a thing that no other work has attempted, and that no other work could do so well.

'Therefore the essential elements of the plan I propose for consideration are these :—

Division of subjects among many specially qualified writers;
Highest pitch of knowledge without the display ;
Distinction between the organic unity of general history
    and the sum of national histories, as the principle for
    selecting and distributing matter ;
Proportion between historic thought and historic fact;
Chart and compass for the coming century.'

The plan outlined in this report received the approval of the Syndics of the Press.   Lord Acton began his editorial work and an announcement of the enterprise was made in *The Athenæum* on 12 December 1896.   But the task was a great one, and, unhappily, Lord Acton did not live to complete it.   In April 1901, when the greater part of the first volume was already in type, serious illness compelled him to put aside his work, and the Syndics, soon afterwards, were constrained to accept, with great reluctance, his decision to relinquish the editorship.   In June 1902, Lord Acton died at Tegernsee in Bavaria.

CHAPTER II.

THE EDITORS AND WRITERS OF THE HISTORY

N Lord Acton's retirement, the Syndics of the Press entrusted the editorship of the *History* to a council of three. Dr A. W. Ward, Master of Peterhouse, formerly Principal and Professor of History in the Owens College, Victoria University, Manchester, was appointed editor-in-chief, with Dr G. W. Prothero, at one time Professor of History in the University of Edinburgh, and Mr Stanley Leathes, Lecturer in History in Trinity College, Cambridge, as his colleagues. Twelve months after their appointment, and some four months after Lord Acton's death, the first volume of *The Cambridge Modern History* saw the light. Under the same editors the work is now approaching completion.

Turning to the writers of the *History*, we find an illustration of the appeal which Lord Acton's scheme made to those who, perhaps, were best able to appreciate its value —his brother historians. The *History*, it will be borne in mind, was to be the original work of the men who knew each part best. Barely two months after the definite adoption of the scheme by the Syndics of the Press, we find Lord Acton reporting the success of his efforts to gather writers who should carry knowledge 'forward across the frontier of the unknown.' Eighty invitations had been sent out, he said, of which ten were still unanswered. Of those who had replied, twelve had refused and fifty-eight had accepted.   So three out of every four of the specialists whom Lord Acton held to be the best qualified, accepted, readily and promptly, his invitation to contribute.

Of this first band of fifty-eight, some fell out, we know, from this cause or that, but the names of the majority are to be found in the following list of writers whose original work, supervised by the editors, forms the volumes actually published of *The Cambridge Modern History*.

THE CAMBRIDGE MODERN HISTORY

WRITERS IN VOLUMES I—IV AND VII—X

Rafael Altamira, *Professor in the University of Oviedo.*
E. Armstrong, *Fellow and Tutor of Queen's College, Oxford.*
Szymon Askenazy, *Professor in the University of Lemberg.*
R. Nisbet Bain, *Assistant Librarian, British Museum.*
Count Ugo Balzani, *of the Reale Accademia dei Lincei.*
William Barry, *D.D.*
The late Mary Bateson, *Lecturer at Newnham College, Cambridge.*
E. A. Benians, *Fellow of St John's College, Cambridge.*
Melville M. Bigelow, *Professor in the Law School, Boston University.*
Lady Blennerhassett.
Émile Bourgeois, *Professor in the University of Paris.*
Émile Boutroux, *Professor in the University of Paris.*
A. G. Bradley, *Trinity College, Cambridge.*
Moritz Brosch, *Ph.D.*
Horatio F. Brown, *LL.D.*
P. Hume Brown, *Professor in the University of Edinburgh.*
Oscar Browning, *University Lecturer in History, Cambridge.*
L. Arthur Burd, *M.A.*
J. B. Bury, *Regius Professor of Modern History, Cambridge.*
A. J. Butler, *Professor of Italian in University College, London.*
J. H. Clapham, *Professor of Economics in the University of Leeds.*
The late H. Butler Clarke, *M.A.*
A. Clutton Brock, *New College, Oxford.*
W. E. Collins, *Bishop of Gibraltar.*
W. J. Courthope, *C.B., D.Litt.*
The late Mandell Creighton, *Bishop of London.*
William Cunningham, *Fellow of Trinity College, Cambridge.*

H. W. C. Davis, *Tutor of Balliol College, Oxford.*
The late John A. Doyle, *Fellow of All Souls College, Oxford.*
R. Dunlop, *M.A.*
R. P. Dunn-Pattison, *Magdalen College, Oxford.*

George Edmundson, *formerly Tutor of Brasenose College, Oxford.*
Hugh E. Egerton, *Beit Professor of Colonial History, Oxford.*
Henry Crosby Emery, *Professor of Political Economy, Yale University.*
A. M. Fairbairn, *Principal of Mansfield College, Oxford.*
J. Neville Figgis, *formerly Birkbeck Lecturer in Ecclesiastical History at Trinity College, Cambridge.*
C. H. Firth, *Regius Professor of Modern History, Oxford.*
H. A. L. Fisher, *Fellow and Tutor of New College, Oxford.*
G. K. Fortescue, *Keeper of Printed Books, British Museum.*

James Gairdner, *C.B., LL.D.*
The late S. R. Gardiner, *Regius Professor of Modern History, Oxford.*
The late Richard Garnett, *Keeper of Printed Books, British Museum.*
G. P. Gooch, *Trinity College, Cambridge.*
Anton Guilland, *Professor of History, Zurich.*

Henry Higgs, *H.M. Treasury.*
Martin Hume, *of the Royal Spanish Academy.*
W. H. Hutton, *Fellow and Tutor of St John's College, Oxford.*

M. R. James, *Provost of King's College, Cambridge.*
The late Sir Richard C. Jebb, *Regius Professor of Greek, Cambridge.*

August Keim, *Major-General in the German Army.*
F. A. Kirkpatrick, *of Trinity College, Cambridge.*
The late F. X. Kraus, *Professor in the University of Freiburg i. Br.*
Sir J. K. Laughton, *Professor of Modern History, King's College, London.*
R. V. Laurence, *Fellow of Trinity College, Cambridge.*
The late Thomas Graves Law, *Librarian at the Signet Library, Edinburgh.*
Henry Charles Lea.
Stanley Leathes, *formerly Fellow of Trinity College, Cambridge.*
Sidney Lee, *Litt.D.*
T. M. Lindsay, *Principal of the Glasgow College of the United Free Church of Scotland.*
E. M. Lloyd, *Colonel R.E.*
Richard Lodge, *Professor of History in the University of Edinburgh.*
J. R. Moreton Macdonald, *of Magdalen College, Oxford.*
J. B. McMaster, *Professor in the University of Pennsylvania.*
The late F. W. Maitland, *Downing Professor of the Laws of England, Cambridge.*
F. C. Montague, *Professor of History in University College, London.*
John B. Moore, *Professor in the Columbia University, New York.*
James Bass Mullinger, *University Lecturer in History, Cambridge.*

J. S. Nicholson, *Professor in the University of Edinburgh.*
The late John G. Nicolay.

C. W. Oman, *Chichele Professor of Modern History, Oxford.*

The late E. J. Payne, *Fellow of University College, Oxford.*
Georges Pariset, *Professor in the University of Nancy.*
Julius von Pflugk-Harttung, *formerly Professor in the University of Basle.*
W. Alison Phillips, *of St John's College, Oxford.*
A. F. Pollard, *Professor in University College, London.*
G. W. Prothero, *formerly Professor of History in the University of Edinburgh.*

W. F. Reddaway, *Fellow of King's College, Cambridge.*
Emil Reich, *Dr. Jur.*
J. G. Robertson, *Professor of German in the University of London.*
J. Holland Rose, *Christ's College, Cambridge.*

John Christopher Schwab, *Professor in Yale University.*
Carlo Segrè, *Professor in the University of Rome.*
W. A. Shaw, *Public Record Office.*
Theodore Clarke Smith, *Assistant Professor, Ohio State University.*
Eugen Stschepkin, *Professor in the University of Odessa.*

J. R. Tanner, *Fellow and Tutor of St John's College, Cambridge.*
H. W. V. Temperley, *Fellow of Peterhouse, Cambridge.*
A. A. Tilley, *Fellow of King's College, Cambridge.*
T. F. Tout, *Professor in the Victoria University, Manchester.*

Paul Viollet, *Professor in the École des Chartes, Paris.*

T. A. Walker, *Fellow and Tutor of Peterhouse, Cambridge.*
A. W. Ward, *Master of Peterhouse, Cambridge.*
Barrett Wendell, *Professor in Harvard University.*
J. P. Whitney, *formerly Principal of the Bishop's College, Lennoxville, Quebec.*
L. G. Wickham Legg, *Lecturer at New College, Oxford.*
P. F. Willert, *Honorary Fellow of Exeter College, Oxford.*
H. W. Wilson, *of Trinity College, Oxford.*
Woodrow Wilson, *President of Princeton University.*

It has been said of *The Cambridge Modern History* that many Universities and two Continents were ransacked for contributors. That the statement is no mere figure of speech is shown by this list of writers, which will be enlarged by that of contributors to the volumes of the work still unpublished. The names it includes—to quote Lord Acton's report—are 'the readers' security for obtaining, without discussion or parade, the most perfect narrative that any English or American scholar can supply.'

CHAPTER III.

THE VALUE OF THE HISTORY

I T is 'modern history that people are ignorant of, and curious about,' wrote Lord Acton to the Syndics of the Press in March 1896. What he meant by *modern* history is best told in his own words, in a passage from his Inaugural Lecture on the Study of History.

'I describe as Modern History,' he then said, 'that which begins four hundred years ago, which is marked off by an evident and intelligible line from the time immediately preceding, and displays in its course specific and distinctive characteristics of its own. The modern age did not proceed from the medieval by normal succession, with outward tokens of legitimate descent. Unheralded, it founded a new order of things, under a law of innovation, sapping the ancient reign of continuity. In those days Columbus subverted the notions of the world, and reversed the conditions of production, wealth, and power; in those days Machiavelli released government from the restraint of law; Erasmus diverted the current of ancient learning from profane into Christian channels; Luther broke the chain of authority and tradition at the strongest link; and Copernicus erected an invincible power that set for ever the mark of progress upon the time that was to come.... The like effects are visible everywhere, and one generation beheld them all.   It was an awakening of new life; the world revolved in a different orbit, determined by influences unknown before.   After many ages persuaded of the headlong decline and impending dissolution of society, and governed by usage and the will of masters who were in their graves, the sixteenth century went forth armed for untried experience, and ready to watch with hopefulness a prospect of incalculable change.   That forward movement divides it broadly from the older world.......

'To men in general I would justify the stress I am laying on Modern History, neither by urging its varied wealth, nor the rupture with precedent, nor the perpetuity of change and increase of pace, nor the growing predominance of opinion over belief, and of knowledge over opinion, but by the argument that it is a narrative told of ourselves, the record of a life which is our own, of efforts not yet abandoned to repose, of problems that still entangle the feet and vex the hearts of men.   Every part of it is weighty with inestimable lessons that we must learn by experience and at a great price, if we know not how to profit by the example and teaching of those who have gone before us, in a society largely resembling the one we live in.   Its study fulfils its purpose even if it only makes us wiser, without producing books, and gives us the gift of historical thinking, which is better than historical learning.'

No words could better express both the interest and the value of the study of modern history.   And the work which Lord Acton himself planned is the only original work in the English language which unfolds, not for one country but for all, that tale told of ourselves, that record of problems still to be solved.

The narrative of *The Cambridge Modern History* is no string of disconnected episodes, but one which displays a continuous development.   From the Middle Ages to the present day, the general history of Europe and her colonies, and of America, is told in twelve volumes, for each of which some historical fact of signal importance is chosen as the central idea, round which individual developments are grouped, not accidentally, but of reasoned purpose. The central facts or figures which thus give to each volume in succession a unity not of name alone, are these :—

I.—THE RENAISSANCE	VII.—THE UNITED STATES
II.—THE REFORMATION	VIII.—THE FRENCH REVOLUTION
III.—THE WARS OF RELIGION	IX.—NAPOLEON
IV.—THE THIRTY YEARS' WAR	X.—THE RESTORATION
V.—THE AGE OF LOUIS XIV	XI.—THE GROWTH OF NATIONALITIES
VI.—THE EIGHTEENTH CENTURY	XII.—THE LATEST AGE

These phrases form the sub-titles of the twelve volumes of text, two of which are published in each year. As regards the order in which they appear, the volumes form two series, corresponding with the two columns above. Thus, the first volume to be published was Volume I, *The Renaissance* ; the second, Volume VII, *The United States*; the third, Volume II, *The Reformation* ; and so on. Under this arrangement eight volumes have now appeared, namely Volumes I, II, III and IV and Volumes VII, VIII, IX and X.

The first of the published volumes of text, *The Renaissance*, includes so much of antecedent history as is necessary for the clear understanding of the conditions with which it is concerned. Each volume contains a full bibliography, a chronological table of leading events and an index. To supplement the narrative, two additional volumes are to be published, making fourteen in all; one to contain *Maps* and the other *Genealogical and other Tables* and a full and detailed *General Index* to the whole work.

Of these supplementary volumes, the first will, it is believed, meet a want which has been very widely expressed. The maps contained in it, now in preparation under the personal supervision of the editors, will show particular countries at successive epochs and will form many series of historical maps of importance and of great illustrative value. They will be mounted, in a separate volume, so as to open flat across both pages of that book; and the reader will thus be able to turn without inconvenience from the page he is reading, in one volume, to the map he wishes to consult, in the other.

We have seen that the aim of *The Cambridge Modern History* is high. Two-thirds of the text have already appeared, and have been reviewed in most of the leading English and American journals, and in many foreign periodicals. *The Cambridge Modern History* is thus not an untried work. The chapter headings from the published volumes may give at least an idea of the way in which historic events are grouped; extracts from the text will show the manner of treatment, while reviews from the public press may serve either to call attention to particular points of interest or to indicate the judgment of the journal from which the quotation is made.

There will be found, on pages 25–32 of the present pamphlet, the chapter headings of Volumes I to IV and VII to X, with a few press notices of each volume. After these, on pages 33–80, ten extracts are given from the text of the *History*. It has been necessary to abbreviate the chapter headings in some instances, while the press notices have had to be confined to a few lines only taken from two or three reviews. The extracts from the text of the *History* itself will, however, be found to be no mere specimen pages, but passages sufficiently full and complete in themselves to afford fair means of judging the value of *The Cambridge Modern History*.

CONTENTS

Volume I.—The Renaissance

Times. Forty years ago it would have been impossible, and twenty years ago it would have been difficult, to find in the United Kingdom a body of scholars who could have dealt with the various problems of European history in the 15th century with anything like the fulness of knowledge exhibited in the volume before us.......
The careful bibliographical list, which will be useful to students as a guide, and to non-students as an indication of the immensity of the range which modern historians must cover, is remarkably complete.

Glasgow Herald. The work deserves high praise and warm welcome as a momentous step in the popularisation of the results of recent historical speculation and research. For a popular work, in the best sense of the term, it is essentially ; although, or rather because, at the same time it is a thorough and scholarly one. Its appeal is not specially to the historical expert, but to the average intelligent, educated man who is a student of history, and has no time or opportunity to go to the original documents.

Guardian. It owes its completion, its editing, and, to some extent, its moulding into form, to the skilful and sympathetic working of three Cambridge scholars—the best historians whom at different dates during comparatively recent years she has produced.......They have had a difficult task and well have they carried it out.

Observer. Chapter after chapter shows the spirit of Renaissance at work in different parts of the civilised world, and in different ways; social, economic, and religious developments are illustrated, and the reader closes the book with a sense of having had the past revealed to him with a new clearness and force. No one who reads this volume but will await with interest its successors, which bid fair to form one of the greatest literary undertakings of the kind; a history that is at once fascinating for the general reader and invaluable for the student, who not only has the history but wonderfully full bibliographies, should he wish further to explore any one of the manifold branches of the great subject.

Volume II.—The Reformation

Daily Chronicle. The Reformation has never been presented with such fulness of knowledge, richness of illustration, absolute fidelity to fact, freedom from bias, and penetrating insight, as in this volume.......Great as the task is of tracing these secular events yet it is accomplished with a completeness of knowledge and perfection of loyalty to truth and fact, that, so far as I know, is not equalled in historical literature. Most cordial thanks are due to the editors and writers for a volume which is sure to take, and likely to keep, the foremost place in the authoritative literature of the Reformation.

Times. It is a volume which is a special justification of Lord Acton's scheme of producing a history by assigning it in portions to various hands. It is scarcely conceivable that a single mind could adequately comprehend or describe the complex movements which made up the Reformation. Dramas of the deepest intensity were simultaneously worked out in the several countries of Europe, and in each country there were circumstances, connected with its past history or its existing characteristics, which gave a peculiar character to its development.......It is the best account of the great century of the Reformation available to English readers.

Daily Mail. A scholarly note runs through the whole of the volume, deeply erudite, deeply sensible, sounded by men of academic learning, with their hearts in their subject and their souls in the movement which revolutionised the ancient religious faith of Europe ; each epoch, and its workers in the supreme struggle, being described by a separate hand. The result is a panorama, moving before the reader, gorgeous with the various colourings of a great battle, whose scenes are laid in different countries.

CONTENTS

Volume III.—The Wars of Religion

Times. As this great work advances it attracts more and more attention. It will soon be in the hands of men, as its founder said, 'grown grey with the dust of archives,' who will prove all things as no reviewer can hope to prove them. But we are confident that those who have organized the endeavour have nothing to fear. Where the standard has been a high one the only anxiety is to improve on what has been done, and future editions, if altered, will but be a good thing bettered.

Daily Chronicle. It is a wonderful repertory of learning and teaching, of sifted evidence and balanced judgment, and belongs distinctly to what the originator of the series called the 'epoch of full-grown history.'......This volume is a most valuable addition to our historical literature, informing, interesting and illuminating; a bright 'lamp shining in a dark place.'

Guardian. We have hitherto had no complete account in English of the extraordinarily complicated events—political, religious, social—which changed the history of Europe and so profoundly affected the future of very many States, between 1525, the Compact of Cracow, and 1621, the death of Philip III of Spain. And here, with admirable lucidity, and in almost every case equally admirable conciseness, we have such an account.......Only a dozen specialists could adequately criticise the work of writers so especially accomplished. Our task must be more general: to express a thorough agreement with the lines taken, and approval of the methods in which each writer has carried out his work. The volume is one of thoroughly good, sound, historical achievement from one end to the other.

Volume IV.—The Thirty Years' War

Athenæum. There is throughout the volume a great deal of special work that demands warm commendation. But even more is praise due to the judgment of authors and editors by which, for the most part, the truly important points are emphasized.......For the most part exactly what should be said is said, and is said accurately.

Scotsman. The editors and those who are cooperating with them have produced a comprehensive history of one of the most intricate and baffling epochs in the progress of civilisation in a manner that redounds to the credit both of those who planned the whole, and of those who have executed the parts.

Daily Mail. Every department of the history is given to some one who has made a special study of that section.......The field of modern history is too vast, and the authorities to be consulted are too many for one man to cover the whole ground of world-history with sufficient thoroughness and impartiality.......For a trustworthy narrative of general history, a combination of specialists under an intelligent body of editors is the only practical method.

CONTENTS

VOLUME VII.—THE UNITED STATES

Bibliographies: Chronological Table of Leading Events: Index.

Spectator. The story of the war as told in this volume by the late Mr John G. Nicolay is, in our judgment, a contribution to modern history of absolutely the first importance. By the premature death of this gifted and judicial writer the world of letters is indeed the poorer. He possessed that gift of selecting and disposing of incidents which is possessed only by the first rank of historians and artists. He knew how to show forth great events and their moving impulses by the presentation of salient characteristics suggestively related, and he never allowed his narrative to be drowned in detail, nor the epic nature of the drama he presented to be obscured by the foam of words. We doubt if the great Civil War will ever be depicted again with such living force as in Mr Nicolay's clear, noble presentment.

Pall Mall Gazette. This volume is a most valuable instalment of the great *Cambridge Modern History.* It is well planned and well carried out. It gives in a brief form, with an exceedingly useful and carefully selected bibliography, the best history of the United States down to the independence of Cuba that has yet appeared on either side of the Atlantic, and not only of the United States, but also of the Dominion down to the permanent establishment of English government.......
The success of this useful undertaking is assured; the public has readily understood the value of Lord Acton's excellent scheme of history; such a volume as this before us can only add largely to its welcome.

Volume VIII.—The French Revolution

Guardian. Now we have entirely what we had wished for—a clear, coherent, well-written, accurate account of the great cataclysm, of its origin, its work, its effects. The tragedy is told in the *Cambridge History* with an admirable dignity, with the true historic feeling, based upon thorough and accurate knowledge....... The point which will strike readers most, we think, is the unity of tone and treatment which belongs to the whole book. There is throughout the same wise, tolerant, moral, emphatic judgment which comes of thorough understanding and sound historical criticism. This admirable spirit is notable everywhere. It is by far the best account of the subject which we possess.

Athenæum. A work of such lasting value and solid scholarship must become a standard authority.

Daily Mail. The *Cambridge Modern History* grows apace, and we begin to realise something of its greatness. Planned by Lord Acton, this library of history could not have had a finer inspiration, and it is no mere compliment to say that Lord Acton's wonderful conception is being wonderfully realised.

CONTENTS

VOLUME IX.—NAPOLEON

Standard. Everyone who wishes to understand where Napoleon triumphed and where he failed, as well as the influence of his life and work, whether in peace or war, on the destinies of mankind, ought to study this admirable and in many respects brilliant ninth volume of *The Cambridge Modern History*......written by experts, English, French, and German, who know how to present the conclusions gained by wide reading and independent thought in a style that is lucid, and with a brevity only possible to scholars who have assimilated their learning....... Unquestionably, this is one of the most interesting and valuable volumes of *The Cambridge Modern History*—a veritable storehouse of information and a trustworthy aid to the interpretation of a dramatic and memorable epoch.

Daily Chronicle. An array of skilfully marshalled facts of the Napoleonic era such as probably has never before been gathered in one volume.

Guardian. The editors of this magnificent work deserve the congratulations of all who are interested in history. Their labours, which must have been immense, have been rewarded by the unstinted praise which has been bestowed on this volume.

Volume X.—The Restoration

As this pamphlet is prepared on the eve of the publication of Volume X, no reviews of that volume are available. So we may pass at once to the last, and perhaps the best, of the means which are here furnished for forming an opinion of the value of *The Cambridge Modern History*—namely, a series of extracts from the published volumes.

Following these passages from the *History*, which occupy the forty-eight pages from page 33 to page 80, there will be found a slight sketch of the interesting history of the Cambridge University Press itself (pages 81–91), some account of the mechanical production of *The Cambridge Modern History* (pages 91–102), and particulars of the various bindings in which the volumes are issued and of the terms on which the *History* may now be obtained (pages 103–106).

THE CAMBRIDGE MODERN HISTORY

THE TRIAL OF SAVONAROLA

(From volume I, chapter V, "Florence: Savonarola," by
E. Armstrong, M.A., Fellow of Queen's College, Oxford)

Neither Savonarola nor the Franciscan challenger, Francesco da Puglia, were the champions of their Orders. Domenico da Pescia, Savonarola's right hand, represented the Dominicans, and Frà Rondinelli the Franciscans. The painful tale of the ordeal is too well known to bear retelling in detail. The Franciscans were gathered in the *Loggia*, and the huge pile was laid in the great *Piazza*, when the Dominicans entered in procession, two by two, amid lines of torch-bearers, followed by Frà Domenico bearing the Host, and his Prior bearing the Crucifix. Their chant "Let God arise and let his enemies be scattered" was caught up by the faithful on every side. The square was free but for the armed bands of the government, and the groups of the leading supporters of each party; but every window and every roof was dark with eager onlookers, hungering for miracles or horrors. Then followed the unseemly wrangles between the Orders, Franciscans insisting that Frà Domenico must be stripped of his robes for fear they should be enchanted, Dominicans refusing to send their champion to the flames without the Host. Then came the drenching thunderstorm, and their wrangles again till eventide, when the *Signoria* dismissed the Friars to their convents. The Dominican procession reached San Marco amid the yells and threats of a disappointed mob.

The populace, long wavering, had made up its mind. Some were angry at their own credulity, others at the proposal to endanger the Holy Sacrament. Many were disgusted at losing a spectacle for which they had waited wet and weary; others had hoped that the Dominican's death by fire would purify the State from faction. Savonarola preached to his disciples that he had won the victory; but in their hearts they doubted it, for they gathered to defend the convent in expectation of an onslaught. This was not slow in coming. On the following day, Palm Sunday, the *Compagnacci* shouted down a Dominican preacher in the cathedral, and amid cries of "To San Marco" led the mob against the convent. Valori escaped to rally adherents round his palace and to attack the enemy from without. But the assailants were too quick; Valori reached his house with difficulty and hid himself; his wife, looking from an upper window, was killed by a cross-bow. Then came officials of the *Signoria* and took him from his hiding-place towards the *Palazzo*. The weak escort was overpowered; a Ridolfi and a Tornabuoni hacked the *Piagnone* leader down, in vengeance for their relation's death, and so the greatest citizen in Florence died unshriven in the street. Meanwhile San Marco was gallantly defended. The bell

was tolling to rally the *Piagnoni*, who, however, were isolated in the
churches or in their houses in blank dismay. Women were gathered in
the nave in prayer, while Savonarola stood before the altar, Sacrament in
hand, with his novices around him, expecting martyrdom, for the convent
doors were burnt and the enemies crowding in. It was high time that
the *Signoria* should interfere in the cause of order. All lay citizens
were commanded on their allegiance to leave the convent within an
hour. Further resistance was hopeless. Savonarola and Frà Domenico
surrendered under promise of safe conduct. For the last time the Prior
gathered the Brethren in the library, and besought them to abide
in faith, in prayer, in patience. The officers led their prisoners out into
the street, and thence to the Palace, through the surging, howling mob,
spitting, kicking and striking at its victims. On the following day
Frà Silvestro left his hiding-place and was given up.

From the moment of Savonarola's arrest, his execution became a
necessity of State; nothing else would satisfy the people, who would
otherwise have clamoured for a proscription of his party; nothing else
would have healed the divisions among the governing class. The
religious strife had not only cleft the city in twain; it was making
her alliance worthless to any foreign power. The news of Charles VIII's
death had arrived, it seemed certain that Pisa could only be recovered
through the League, and this would give no aid while Savonarola
thundered from the pulpit against the Pope. Exile was an alternative
to death, but exile would have removed the danger to a foreign and
almost necessarily hostile State; the *Piagnoni* would never rest, while
there was a possibility of their leader's return. The Pope at once
urged the transference of the prisoner to Rome; the government, as a
reward for silencing the prophet, pressed for a tithe upon the clergy for
the Pisan war. Florentine independence declined to play the sheriff's
officer for Rome, and Savonarola's extradition was refused; as a compromise the Pope sent commissioners to aid in his examination.

The trial of the three Friars lasted from April 9 until May 22.
Their depositions and those of other citizens are not necessarily worthless,
because they were extracted under torture. Torture was invariably
applied, and such a view would invalidate, for instance, the whole of
the evidence on which the Medicean conspirators were condemned.
Savonarola was, however, a bad subject. His nervous, highly-strung
constitution, weakened by asceticism and anxiety, shrank from physical
pain. Though never abandoning his duty, he had always been haunted
by the fear of personal violence; he frequently referred to his providential escapes from the poison or the dagger of Ludovico *il Moro*,
although successive governments devoted to the Friar never contrived
to arrest one of these Milanese agents, with whom he believed Florence
to be teeming. The prosecution admitted that Savonarola retracted the
confessions made under torture, and these retractations are set down in

black and white. Not all of the Florentine commission were pronounced enemies; and of the two papal commissioners, the General of the Dominicans, Turriani, had, until Savonarola's final act of disobedience, been his consistent friend. More difficult is the question of the additions, alterations, and omissions attributed to the notary Ser Ceccone, a renegade; although, had this "editing" been absolutely unscrupulous, the confessions of the accused would have been more compromising. The depositions of Frà Domenico, whether in their original form or in the official copy, bear out the general authenticity of the evidence, as do even those of the hysterical somnambulist Frà Silvestro, who was believed by many to be more knave than fool, and with whom, it was suspected, the less scrupulous leaders of the *Piagnoni* conducted their political correspondence.

The Florentine commissioners directed the examination mainly to the gift of prophecy and political relations. It was essential to extort from Savonarola a denial of his prophecies; for nothing would so effectually alienate the large numbers who still silently clung to him. At first he stoutly asserted the divine origin of his gift, but under the strain of torture he broke down, and henceforth his answers were contradictory or confused. He was perhaps at war within himself on this mysterious subject, on which even his pulpit utterances are not consistent; in his agony of mind he now cried out that the spirit of prophecy had departed from him. The prosecution represented him as admitting that his alleged gift was an imposture, the result of ambition, of the desire to be thought wise and holy. He strenuously denied that his prophecies were founded on confessions made to Frà Silvestro or himself. With regard to his interference in party politics the depositions of the three Friars were very colourless. It was the wish of the government to narrow the issue to San Marco, and not to mark leading citizens out for popular vengeance. Even those who were arrested and tortured were soon released. Not Savonarola's old aristocratic enemies, but the people were the most vindictive. Parenti, whose own opinions are typical of the changes in public feeling, affirms that, to satisfy the people and to save the heads of the Savonarola party, the government replaced four of the Friar's judges, who might possibly be too favourable to his cause. The aristocracy could escape a revolution only by his condemnation. Valori and his associates, it was confessed, frequently visited the convent, as did other believers high and low; the Friars had heard their visitors speak of the prospects of the coming elections; their prayers had been sometimes asked in the cause of righteousness, but there had been nothing in the nature of an electoral organisation. Savonarola clearly avowed that he had supported the popular government, but had not meddled with its workings. Both he and Frà Domenico mentioned their design for a life-Gonfalonier or Doge. Their thoughts had naturally turned to Valori, but his violent and eccentric character made them hesitate; the excellent Giovanni Battista Ridolfi had been mentioned, but his large family connexion might lead to the predominance of a single house; Savonarola had protested against the tendency to form an oligarchical ring within his party. In all this there was no implication of any political association, nothing to compel the *Signoria* to extend enquiry further.

On the arrival of the papal commissioners the examination turned on Savonarola's appeal to a General Council; it was conducted chiefly by the Spanish lawyer Romolino, Bishop of Ilerda. Savonarola confessed that, having no friend in Italy, he had turned to foreign princes, and especially to those of France and Spain: he hoped for the aid of Cardinals Brissonet and della Rovere, both enemies of the Borgia; Matthæus Lang, Maximilian's confidential adviser (afterwards Bishop of Gurk and Cardinal), had spoken ill of Alexander in the Friar's presence, while the scandals of the Curia were odious to the Spanish sovereigns who could influence the Cardinal of Lisbon. In vain the commissary pressed for evidence to implicate the Cardinal of Naples; for confessions extracted by torture were afterwards withdrawn. The victim declared that he had no wish to be Pope or Cardinal; his reward would be enough, if by his agency so glorious a work as the reform of the Church could be effected.

Extorted and garbled as they were, these depositions showed no proof, in Guicciardini's words, of any fault except ambition. And who can say that in his last agony Savonarola himself may not have been conscious of past ambition, of the parasite which clings most closely to monastic walls? Pride was the fault which from the first Alexander VI had fixed on his future enemy.

The result of the trial was less the condemnation of Savonarola than that of the popular government on which he had pinned his faith. It would be vain to seek under Medici or Albizzi so violent a strain on the constitution, so shameless a disregard for individual rights. It was pitiful that the free constitution, the panacea against tyranny, should have been guilty of the worst crime with which Florence can be charged. Of physical or political courage there was none, save in the small band which in the heat of fight had held the convent. Only a short time before, the Milanese ambassador had assured his master that Savonarola controlled the great majority of the town; yet now no *Piagnone* dared mention his prophet in the streets. The Eight and the Ten were known to have Savonarolist sympathies; in defiance of the most fundamental constitutional traditions, without even the pretence of a *Balìa*, they were dismissed before their office had expired. There was no protest from these lawfully elected bodies, and none from the Council which had given them their commission. When the new *Signoria* was elected, the well-known *Piagnoni* were forcibly excluded; the qualification for office became cowardice or party hate. The Council itself suffered the garbled depositions to be read, and did not insist on the appearance of the accused, because a *Signoria*, notoriously hostile, stated that he was voluntarily absent from fear of stoning. In the Council and in the magistracies, Savonarola, as was afterwards proved, must have numbered hundreds of secret adherents. Yet one citizen only, Agnolo Niccolini, dared to suggest that death should be commuted for perpetual imprisonment, so that posterity might not lose the fruits of the invaluable works which Savonarola might write in prison. The Florentine constitution was still a sham; there was still no correspondence between real and nominal power; the mandatories of the people were swayed by a ferocious faction, as they had been swayed by a cool-headed dynasty. It is small wonder that the hybrid constitution withered in the first fierce heat; that when a few thousand famished Spaniards rushed the walls of Prato, two audacious youths dragged the chief magistrate of the Florentine Republic from the *Palazzo Pubblico*, and condescendingly gave him their escort to his home.

In the sentence pronounced on May 22, 1498, Church and State concurred. Savonarola and his companions were declared heretics and schismatics, because they had denied that Alexander was true Pope and had compassed his deposition; because they had distorted Scripture and had revealed the secrets of the confessional under the pretext that they were vouchsafed by visions. Against the State they had sinned in causing the useless expenditure of countless treasure and the death of many innocent citizens, and in keeping the city divided against herself. Unity between the city and the Pope was now complete; Florence obtained the grant of three-tenths of Church revenues; the price, observed the *Piagnoni*, of them that sold innocent blood was three times ten. Even to the three Friars Alexander sent his absolution. On the morrow came the end. Unfrocked and degraded by the Archbishops Suffragan, condemned as heretics and schismatics by the papal commissaries, Savonarola and his Brethren were handed over to the secular arm, the Eight, who passed the formal sentence. Led from the *ringhiera* along a raised platform to the scaffold, they were hanged from the gibbet, and when life was extinct the pile was lit. The boys of Florence stoned the bodies as they hung. Four years ago they had stoned Piero de' Medici; then, in an access of righteousness, they had stoned notorious sinners. Now they stoned their prophet, and lastly they were to stone to death his executioner. The bodies were cut down into the flames, the ashes carefully collected and thrown into the Arno. The *Piazza* had been thronged with onlookers, for whom barrels were broached and food provided at government expense. For the crowd it was a vast municipal picnic; the burning of the Friars replaced the burning of the Vanities, even as this had superseded the fireworks and pageants of the Medici.

THE NEW WORLD AND ITS GOLD

(From volume I, chapter XV, " Economic Change," by
W. Cunningham, D.D., Fellow of Trinity College, Cambridge)

The discovery of America by Colombo gave the Spaniards access to
an enormous territory of which they were complete masters, and which
they were free to develop on any lines that seemed good to them. It is
no part of our present purpose to discuss by itself the colonial policy
which the monarchs followed; we have rather to consider the aims pursued
by them for their empire as a whole. The large mass of bullion that
was imported, together with the great commercial opportunities that were
opened up, exercised a remarkable influence upon economic conditions in
the peninsula. The amount of gold and silver which the Spaniards
acquired was quite unprecedented, and might have been used to form
a very large capital indeed. The West India islands supplied increasing
quantities of gold from the time of their discovery until 1516. In 1522
the exploitation of Mexico began; silver was acquired in greater and
greater masses, and the introduction, in 1557, of a simpler process of
reduction of the ore by means of quicksilver diminished the cost of
production and still farther augmented the yield of bullion. In 1533
the Spaniards also obtained access to Peru, from which additional
supplies of silver were procured. Altogether, an enormous stream of
bullion poured into Spain during the whole of the sixteenth century.

The Spaniards were able to rely on the best possible advice as to the
organisation of business of every kind. Genoese financiers were ready
to give every assistance, and the South-German capitalists, who had
so much experience of mining and enterprise of every sort, were closely
attached to the interests of Charles V; after his accession to the throne
of Spain they were attracted to that country in large numbers, as great
privileges were conferred upon them. They were able to take part
in colonisation, and to engage directly in mining. The Fuggers
undertook to develop the quicksilver deposits of Almaden; they formed
business connexions in the New World, and founded settlements in
Peru. The Welsers established a colony in Venezuela, and undertook
copper-mining in San Domingo. There was at the same time an
incursion, chiefly to Seville, of other German capitalists, who were
prepared to devote their energies to developing the industrial arts
of Spain. With all these material and technical advantages it seems
extraordinary that the dreams of Charles V and Philip II were not
realised, and that they failed to build up such a military power as
would have enabled them to establish a complete supremacy in
Europe.

It would be exceedingly interesting if we were able to examine in
detail the extent to which the precious metals came into circulation in
Spain, and the precise course of economic affairs in different parts of the

country; but the material for such an enquiry does not appear to be forthcoming. Yet one thing is obvious; the Spanish colonists devoted themselves almost entirely to mining for the precious metals, and they were largely dependent for their supply of food of all kinds on the mother country. This caused an increased demand for corn in Spain and a rapid rise of prices there, as the colonists were able to pay large sums for the necessaries of life. Charles V, indeed, endeavoured to carry out works of irrigation, and to increase the food-supply by bringing a larger area under cultivation. But tillage could not be developed so as to meet the new demands. The methods of cultivation already in vogue were as high as was generally practicable in the existing state of society; the vine- and olive-growers on the one hand, and the pasture-farmers on the other, resented any encroachments on the land at their disposal, so that it was impossible to bring a larger area under crop. So powerful were the *Mesta*, a great corporation of sheep-farmers, that they were actually able in 1552 to insist that Crown- and Church-land which had been brought under tillage should revert to pasture. The result was inevitable; food became dearer, and the government was forced to recognise the fact by raising the *maximum* limit of price; as a consequence, the necessary outlay of all classes increased, while a large part of the population were not compensated by the profit obtained through the new facilities for trade.

Under ordinary circumstances the increase in the price of food would have been merely injurious to industry; it would necessitate a larger outlay in the expenses of production, and would leave less margin for profit, and no opportunity for the formation of capital. Ultimately, this seems to have been the effect on Spanish manufactures, and the high cost of production in the peninsula rendered it possible for other European countries, where the range of prices was lower, to undersell the Spanish producer in the home market. No serious attempt was made by the government to check this tendency, as the policy pursued was in the main that of favouring the consumer, and protective tariffs were not introduced.

The circumstances which prevailed in Spain at the opening of the sixteenth century were, however, quite exceptional, and as a matter of fact there seems to have been a considerable, though short-lived, development of industry. The colonists not only imported their food, but manufactures as well; there was a sudden increase in the demand both for textile goods and for hardware, to meet the American requirements, and of course there was a great rise of prices. The small independent masters, working on the old industrial system, were unable to cope with this new state of affairs; but the foreign capitalists saw their opportunity. Manufacturing of every kind was organised on a large scale at Toledo and other centres; wages rose enormously, and a great influx of population was attracted into the city. This was doubtless drawn to some extent from the rural districts; but the stream must have been considerably augmented by the immigration of French and Italians. Hence it appears that this rapid industrial development was merely an excrescence, which had no very deep attachment to the country; the Spaniards themselves appear to have regarded it as an intrusion, and to have resented it accordingly. The Spanish gentry had no means of paying the increased prices which the colonial demand had occasioned, for natural economy was still in vogue in many rural districts. Indeed, this revolution in industry must have given rise to many social grievances; the craftsman of the old school would suffer from the competition of the capitalist in his own trade, while the great rise of prices to consumers was attributed to the greed of the foreigner. The government was persuaded to pass measures which imposed disabilities on foreign capitalists; it succeeded in forcing the withdrawal of the French and Italian workmen, as well as in expelling the *Moriscos.* As these changes ensued, the foreign capitalists were doubtless successful in transferring large portions of their capital to other lands; but the decline of alien competition on Spanish soil did not enable native manufacturers to take their place or to recover the lost ground. With the new scale of outlay they had little opportunity for forming capital, and the *bourgeois* class may not have had the skill for organising business on the new lines. On the whole it appears that the large colonial demands for food on the one hand, and the large supplies of foreign manufactures on the other, prevented a healthy reaction of commercial on agricultural and industrial development; Spain was left exhausted by the feverish activity which had been temporarily induced, and which passed away.

The Spanish government was firmly convinced that the best means of promoting the power of the country was by hoarding the large share of the produce of the mines which came into their possession, and they made frequent efforts to prevent the export of any bullion into other parts of Europe, though the Genoese and German capitalists had special licenses which allowed them to transmit it. It is obviously impossible that the government could have succeeded in enforcing this prohibition, under the existing conditions of trade; most of the bullion which arrived at Seville belonged to the merchants and manufacturers who were concerned in supplying the colonial demand for goods. The ingots which were not taken to the mint may have been hoarded for a time; but the foreign capitalists would not allow their money to lie idle, and much of it must have been exported, in spite of all laws to the contrary, to pay for the cheaper manufactures which were coming in from abroad. Comparatively little coin could have passed into general circulation in Spain itself; payments from the towns for agricultural produce would scarcely overbalance the payments due from the country for the dearer manufactured goods.

The Spanish rulers had ignorantly and unintentionally pursued the precise course of policy recommended by Machiavelli. They had sought to accumulate treasure in the coffers of the State, and they had by their mistaken measures allowed the subjects to continue poor. The wealth which passed into the country had no steady and persistent reaction on industrial and agricultural life; and when the military exigencies of Philip's policy reduced him to bankruptcy, it became obvious to the world that the Spaniards had completely misused the unique opportunities which lay within their grasp. They had sacrificed everything else to the accumulation of treasure by the Crown, and they had completely failed to attain the one object on which they had concentrated all their efforts.

The permanent gain from the treasure imported into Europe went to those countries which were able to employ it as capital for industrial or agricultural improvement, and Spain could do neither. There was every prospect, at one time, that the greatest advantage would be reaped by Spanish subjects in the Netherlands. The policy of the government, however, and the failure of the Duke of Alva to recognise the importance of trading interests, rendered this impossible. The War in the Low Countries not only caused the migration of industry from that part of Spanish territory, but tended to bring about the collapse of the great capitalists who had allied themselves to the Spanish interest. The foreigners were being gradually excluded from taking any direct part in the new industrial developments in Spain; they confined themselves more and more to banking business, and to financial operations in the government service. But the persistent failure of the Spanish and imperial policy in one country after another had the effect of crippling several of the great Genoese and German houses, and at length drained the resources even of such millionaires as the Fuggers. The decline of these bankers proved that the control of the treasure of the New World was passing into other hands; as a matter of fact it was shifting more and more into the possession of the Dutch, who were making their country a harbour of refuge for persons expelled from the Spanish Netherlands, and who were building up a great centre of commercial and industrial life at Amsterdam. At the beginning of the seventeenth century the people of Holland had succeeded in winning the greater part of the gains which accrued from the Portuguese discoveries, while they had also succeeded in drawing to themselves a large share of the treasure of Spanish America, and in using it as capital in commerce, in shipping, and in industrial pursuits. It was the nemesis of the policy of his Catholic Majesty that his subjects failed to derive real advantage from the much vaunted American possessions, and that the gains which might have enriched the peninsula went to his bitterest enemies.

MARTIN LUTHER AND THE DIET OF WORMS

(From volume II, chapter IV, "Luther," by T. M. Lindsay, D.D., Principal of the Glasgow College of the United Free Church of Scotland)

The Appeal *To the Christian Nobility of the German Nation* made the greatest immediate impression. Contemporaries called it a trumpet blast. It was a call to all Germany to unite against Rome. It was written in haste, but must have been long meditated upon. Luther wrote the introduction on the 23rd of June (1520); the printers worked as he wrote; it was finished and published about the middle of August, and by the 18th of the month 4000 copies had gone into all parts of Germany and the printers could not supply the demand. This Appeal was the manifesto of a revolution sent forth by a true leader of men, able to concentrate the attack and direct it to the enemy's one vital spot. It grasped the whole situation; it summed up with vigour and directness all the grievances which had hitherto been stated separately and weakly; it embodied every proposal of reform, however incomplete, and set it in its proper place in one combined scheme. All the parts were welded together by a simple and direct religious faith, and made living by the moral earnestness which pervaded the whole.

Reform had been impossible, the Appeal says, because the walls behind which Rome lay entrenched had been left standing—walls of straw and paper, but in appearance formidable fortifications. If the temporal Powers demanded reforms, they were told that the Spiritual Power was superior and controlling. If the Spiritual Power itself was attacked from the side of Scripture, it was affirmed that no one could say what Scripture really meant but the Pope. If a Council was called for to make the reform, men were informed that it was impossible to summon a Council without the leave of the Pope. Now this pretended Spiritual Power which made reform impossible was a delusion. The only real spiritual power existing belonged to the whole body of believers in virtue of the spiritual priesthood bestowed upon them by Christ Himself. The clergy were distinguished from the laity, not by an indelible character imposed upon them in a divine mystery called ordination, but because they were set in the commonwealth to do a particular work. If they neglected the work they were there to do, the clergy were accountable to the same temporal Powers which ruled the land. The statement that the Pope alone can interpret Scripture is a foolish one; the Holy Scripture is open to all, and can be interpreted by all true believers who have the mind of Christ and come to the Word of God humbly and really seeking enlightenment. When a Council is needed, every individual Christian has a right to do his best to get it summoned, and the temporal Powers are there to represent and enforce his wishes.

The straw walls having been cleared away, the Appeal proceeds with an indictment against Rome.   There is in Rome one who calls himself the Vicar of Christ and whose life has small resemblance to that of our Lord and St Peter; for this man wears a triple crown (a single one does not content him), and keeps up such a state that he requires a larger personal revenue than the Emperor.   He has surrounding him a number of men called Cardinals, whose only apparent use is to draw to themselves the revenues of the richest convents and benefices and to spend this money in keeping up the state of a wealthy monarch in Rome.   In this way, and through other holders of German benefices who live as hangers-on at the papal court, Rome takes from Germany a sum of 300,000 gulden annually,—more than is paid to the Emperor.   Rome robs Germany in many other ways, most of them fraudulent—*annates*, absolution money, &c.   The chicanery used to get possession of German benefices; the exactions on the bestowal of the *pallium*; the trafficking in exemptions and permissions to evade laws ecclesiastical and moral, are all trenchantly described. The plan of reform sketched includes the complete abolition of the supremacy of the Pope over the State; the creation of a national German Church with an ecclesiastical national Council, to be the final court of appeal for Germany and to represent the German Church as the Diet did the German State; some internal religious reforms, such as the limitation of the number of pilgrimages, which are destroying morality and creating in men a distaste for honest work; reductions in the mendicant Orders, which are mere incentives to a life of beggary; the inspection of all convents and nunneries and permission given to those who are dissatisfied with their monastic lives to return to the world; the limitation of ecclesiastical festivals which are too often nothing but scenes of gluttony, drunkenness, and debauchery; a married priesthood and an end put to the universal and degrading concubinage of the German parish priests. The Appeal closes with some solemn words addressed to the luxury and licensed immorality of the cities.

None of Luther's writings produced such an instantaneous, widespread, and powerful effect as did this Appeal.   It went circulating all over Germany, uniting all classes of society in a way hitherto unknown. It was an effectual antidote, so far as the majority of the German people was concerned, to the Bull of Excommunication which had been prepared in Rome by Cajetan, Prierias, and Eck, and had been published there in June, 1520.   Eck was entrusted with the publication of the Bull in Germany, where it did not command much respect.   It had been drafted by men who had been Luther's opponents, and suggested the gratification of private animosity rather than calm judicial examination and rejection of heretical opinion.   The feeling grew stronger when it was discovered that Eck, having received the power to do so, had inserted the names of Adelmann, Pirkheimer, Spengler, and Carlstadt along with that of Luther—all five personal enemies. The German Bishops seemed to be unwilling to allow the publication of the Bull within their districts. Later the publication became dangerous, so threatening was the attitude of the crowds. Luther, on his part, burnt the Bull publicly; and electrified Germany by the deed. Rome had now done its utmost to get rid of Luther by way of ecclesiastical repression. If he was to be overthrown, if the new religious movement and the national uprising which enclosed it, were to be stifled, this could only be done by the aid of the highest secular power. The Roman Curia turned to the Emperor.

Maximilian had died suddenly on the 12th of January, 1519. After some months of intriguing, the papal diplomacy being very tortuous, his grandson, Charles V, the young King of Spain, was unanimously chosen to be his successor (June 28). Troubles in Spain prevented him from leaving that country at once to take possession of his new dignities. He was crowned at Aachen on the 23rd of October, 1520, and opened his first German Diet on January 22, 1521.

The proceedings of this Diet were of great importance apart from its relation to Luther; but to the common people of Germany, to the papal Nuncios, Aleander and Caraccioli, and to the foreign envoys, the issues raised by Luther's revolt against Rome were the matters of absorbing interest. Girolamo Aleander had been specially selected by Pope Leo X to secure Luther's condemnation by the Emperor. He was a cultivated Churchman, who knew Germany well, and had been in intimate relations with many of the German humanists. His despatches and those of the envoys of England, Spain, and Venice witness to the extraordinary excitement among the people of all classes. Aleander had been in Germany ten years earlier, and had found no people so devoted to the Papacy as the Germans. Now all things were changed. The legion of poor nobles, the German lawyers and canonists, the professors and students, the men of learning and the poets, were all on Luther's side. Most of the monks, a large portion of the clergy, many of the Bishops, supported Luther. His friends had the audacity to establish a printing-press in Worms, whence issued quantities of the forbidden writings, which were hawked about in the market-place, on the streets, and even within the Emperor's palace. These books were eagerly bought and read with avidity; large prices were sometimes given for them.

Aleander could not induce the Emperor to consent to Luther's immediate condemnation. Charles must have felt the difficulties of the situation. His position as head of the Holy Roman Empire, the traditional policy of the Habsburg family, his own deeply rooted personal convictions, which found outcome in the brief statement read to the Princes on the day after Luther's appearance, all go to prove that he had not the slightest sympathy with the Reformer and that he had resolved that he should be condemned. But the Diet's consent was necessary before the imperial ban could be issued; and besides Charles had his own bargain to make with the Pope, and this matter of Luther might help him to make a good one. The Diet resolved that Luther should be heard; a safe-conduct was sent along with the summons to attend; Luther travelled to Worms in what seemed like a triumphal procession to the angry partisans of the Pope; and on April 16th he appeared before Charles and the Diet. He entered smiling, says Aleander; he looked slowly round the assembly and his face became grave. On a table near where he was placed there was a pile of books. Twenty-five of Luther's writings had been hastily collected by command of the Emperor and placed there. The procedure was entrusted to John Eck, the Official of Trier (to be distinguished from John Eck of Ingolstadt), a man in whom Aleander had much confidence and who was lodged, he says significantly, in the chamber next his. Luther was asked whether the books before him were of his authorship (the names were read over to him), and whether he would retract what he had written in them. He answered, acknowledging the books, but asked for time to consider how to reply to the second question. He was granted delay till the following day; and retired to his lodging.

The evening and the night were a time of terrible depression, conflict, despair, and prayer. Before the dawn came the victory had been won, and he felt in a great calm. He was sent for in the evening (April 18); the streets were so thronged that his conductors had to take him by obscure passages to the Diet. There was the same table with the same pile of books. This time Luther was ready with his answer, and his voice had recovered its clear musical note. When asked whether, having acknowledged the books to be his, he was prepared to defend them or to withdraw them, he replied at some length. In substance, it was, that his books were not all of the same kind: in some he had written on faith and morals in a way approved by all, and that it was needless to retract what friends and foes alike approved of; others were written against the Papacy, a system which by teaching and example was ruining Christendom, and that he could not retract these writings; as for the rest, he was prepared to admit that he might have been more violent in his charges than became a Christian, but still he was not prepared to retract them either; but he was ready to listen to anyone who could show that he had erred. The speech was repeated in Latin for the benefit of the Emperor. Then Charles told him through Eck that he was not there to question matters which had been long ago decided and settled by General Councils, and that he must answer plainly whether he meant to retract what he had said contradicting the decisions of the Council of Constance. Luther answered that he must be convinced by Holy Scripture, for he knew that both Pope and Councils had erred; his conscience was fast bound to Holy Scripture, and it was neither safe nor honest to act against conscience. This was said in German and in Latin. The Emperor asked him, through Eck, whether he actually believed that a General Council could err. Luther replied that he did, and could prove it. Eck was about to begin a discussion, but Charles interposed. His interest was evidently confined to the one point of a General Council. Luther was dismissed, the crowd followed him, and a number of the followers of the Elector of Saxony accompanied him. Aleander tells us that as he left the audience hall he raised his hand in the fashion of the German soldier who had struck a good stroke. He had struck his stroke, and left the hall.

Next day Charles met the princes, and read them a paper in which he had written his own opinion of what ought to be done. The Germans pleaded for delay and negotiations with Luther. This was agreed to, and meetings were held in hopes of arriving at a conference. A commission of eight, representing the Electors, the nobles, and the cities, was appointed to meet with Luther. They were all sincerely anxious to arrive at a working compromise; but the negotiations were in vain. The Emperor's assertion of the infallibility of a General Council, and Luther's phrase, a conscience fast bound to the Holy Scripture, could not be welded together by any diplomacy however sincere. The Word of God was to Luther a living voice speaking to his own soul; it was not to be stifled by the decisions of any Council; Luther was ready to lay down his life, rather than accept any compromise which endangered the Christian liberty which came to men by justifying faith.

The negotiations having failed, the Ban of the Empire was pronounced against Luther. It was dated on the day on which Charles concluded his secret treaty with Pope Leo X, as if to make clear to the Pope the price which he paid for the condemnation of the Reformer. Luther was ordered to quit Worms on April 26th, and his safe-conduct protected him for twenty days, and no longer. At their expiration he was liable to be seized and destroyed as a pestilent heretic. On his journey homewards he was captured by a band of soldiers and taken to the Castle of the Wartburg by order of the Elector of Saxony. This was his " Patmos," where he was to be kept in safety until the troubles were over. His disappearance did not mean that he was no longer a great leader of men ; but it marks the time when the Lutheran revolt merges in national opposition to Rome.

THE SPANISH ARMADA

(From volume III, chapter IX, "The Elizabethan Naval War with Spain," by J. K. Laughton, M.A., Professor of Modern History, King's College, London)

Immediately the Armada put to sea, its troubles began. The weather was boisterous; and the ships, built and rigged for fine weather passages, with a fair, equable wind, to or from the West Indies, were overmasted and undermanned. The seamen were also of very indifferent quality, being, in great measure, mere fair-weather sailors. The ships made very bad weather, were strained, leaked excessively; some were dismasted, all were reduced to a deplorable condition, which the sea-sick soldiers thought worse than it really was. Their victuals, too, failed: the bread was mouldy, the meat was putrid, the water-casks—made of green staves—leaked, and the water ran short. Sickness broke out among the men, and Medina Sidonia considered himself lucky in getting the bulk of his fleet safely into Corunna, where he anchored on June 9, but in such distress and confusion that he made no general signal, and took no pains to let distant ships know what he was doing; so that many kept on their way to the appointed rendezvous, south of the Scilly Islands, whence they were recalled, but not before they had been seen and reported, on June 19, by some English traders. He was not able to sail again till July 12.

Meantime Howard, with the English fleet at Plymouth, had been very anxious to visit the coast of Spain and work such havoc among the enemy's shipping that their design would have to be again postponed, if not altogether abandoned. This seemed particularly easy when it was known that they were congregated in the harbour of Corunna; and it now appears quite certain that an onslaught there, such as Drake had made at Cadiz the previous year, guided by the experience then gained and supported by a few fire-ships, would have utterly ruined the Spanish navy. But Elizabeth would not allow the attempt to be made. She professed to doubt whether the Armada was really coming; she affected to consider that the differences between the two nations might be settled by negotiation. Whether she hoped to hoodwink Philip, or whether she imagined that, if not further provoked, he would allow the war to conduct itself in the same semi-private, piratical, and economical way as during the last ten years, it is impossible to say; or may be she really believed that the danger of missing the Armada was too great; that if it had already put to sea it might be stretching to the westward while the English were crossing the Bay of Biscay; and might, without opposition, come into the Channel and off Dunkirk, while

Howard or Drake was searching the Spanish coast from Corunna to Cadiz. She turned a deaf ear to the arguments of Howard and his council of war, and peremptorily ordered him not to go beyond Ushant.

Another and very pressing anxiety that filled Howard's mind was the frequently occurring want of victuals. There was no public store ready to hand; and the sudden call to supply a force numbering some 15,000 men taxed the energies of the victualling agents. By the utmost economy and putting the men on short allowance he managed to get together what might be called a private stock against an emergency; but whilst in the Narrow Sea, and afterwards, at Plymouth, he never ceased urging on the Queen's ministers the necessity for liberal supplies. It does not appear that there was any undue sparing of expense, though there was, of course, a strict attention to economy; but it was impossible to provide the larger supplies which Howard demanded. The practice, so far as there was one, was to send at one time victuals for four weeks, and to replenish them by another supply for four weeks about a week before the earlier supply was exhausted. There was thus, as Howard pointed out, the continually recurring danger of the fleet being obliged to put to sea, in presence of the enemy, with not more than a few days' victuals on board. This was what did actually happen. The fleet had been out, spreading in a long line from Ushant to Scilly, when a fresh southerly wind blew it back to Plymouth. The victuals were running low and the ships busy provisioning, when, on July 19, the Armada was reported off the Lizard. The same southerly wind which drove the English fleet in, had carried the Spanish straight across the Bay of Biscay. The fresh breeze had, however, been too much for them. The ships were scattered; many had parted company, and it was not till the next day, July 20, that they had nearly all rejoined.

In accordance with the custom very generally followed in an age when the commander-in-chief of a fleet was often regarded as a president and moderator rather than as actual commander, and especially necessary under the conditions existing among the Spaniards, a council of war was held, but was unable to decide anything for want of intelligence. A proposal to look into Plymouth and attack the English fleet came to nothing, because it was not known whether it was there or not. In the afternoon they saw some ships under the land, but the weather was thick, with rain and mist, and they could not make out either their number or quality. It was not till night had fallen that one of the pinnaces picked up an English boat, and the Duke learned from the prisoners that the English fleet had been at Plymouth but had got to sea that afternoon. Their ships had, in fact, warped out into the Sound on the evening of the 19th; on the 20th they had plied out, to windward, against a fresh south-westerly breeze; and the Armada, running to the eastward all night, had by daybreak on the 21st given the English the weather-gage for which they had been working. The fleet with Howard at this time consisted of about seventy ships, a large proportion of which were small coasting vessels, useful as cruisers, as scouts, or to carry messages, but of little fighting value. Thirty of them belonged to the Queen; and of these, thirteen, though on the average smaller than the best of the Spaniards, were more heavily armed. Some seven or eight more were good and efficient ships, of a smaller size, but still heavily armed in comparison with the Spanish ships; and about a dozen or twenty of the merchantmen were sufficiently large and well armed to be able to take part in an engagement. This estimate shows the number of fighting ships in the two fleets to have not been very unequal; those on each side being superior to those of the enemy from their own special point of view; though, indeed, if the Spaniards could have dictated the manner of fighting, they would have had upwards of sixty effective ships, and their superiority would have been overwhelming. They themselves thought that it was; and what they believed was the general belief throughout Europe. In reality, the superiority to which they trusted was more than nullified by the hopeless inferiority of their ships and their seamen; it depended entirely on their being able to close with and grapple the English ships, and this they could never succeed in doing. The English ships of the new design had finer lines and were much faster; they were lower in the water, and were stiffer and more weatherly; they were rigged and were manned by seamen accustomed to the boisterous weather of the higher latitudes. The choice of the fighting rested with them; and with that, also the superiority. The Spanish ships were so crank that, in a fresh breeze, their weather guns sent their shot flying through empty space or their lee guns plumped them into the sea, whilst the English, on a more even keel, racked the Spaniards through and through below the water line on the one side, or swept their decks with a murderous hail on the other. They could take their own distance; and, when the Spaniards tried to close, could slip away from them with an ease that astonished and terrified their enemy.

At the first meeting of the two fleets on the forenoon of July 21 all this was at once apparent. To Drake and many of the others it was no new thing, though it is probable that even they had not realised how vast their advantage was. The fight continued from nine o'clock to about one, when Medina Sidonia, discovering that it was only wasting time, and that he was bound to avoid all delay, made sail before the wind. It was a fatal mistake—one we may be sure that Santa Cruz would not have made. He might not, probably would not, have been able to neutralise the vast superiority of the English ships and the English method of fighting; but it is not conceivable that a man of his experience would have jumbled the transports, store-ships, and fighting ships in one heterogeneous crowd, or would have sought a pretext of flying before the enemy from a half-finished battle. As it was, the fighting on July 21 gave the keynote to all that followed. The Armada was to hurry on. The flag-ship of Pedro de Valdes, which had suffered severely in the engagement, lost her foremast by a collision with another of her squadron and fell astern. But time could not be wasted in defending the noblest ship in the fleet; she was deserted and fell into the hands of the English. Another, the vice-admiral of Oquendo's squadron, was disabled by an accidental explosion of powder; she, too, was deserted, was taken by the English and sent to Weymouth. And ever the Armada sailed heavily on with a fresh fair wind, the English following, ready to seize on any stragglers, or to fight if opportunity offered. There was thus a smart action off St Alban's Head on the 23rd, and another on the 25th off St Catherine's in the Isle of Wight, as a visible result of which a third large ship, Recalde's flag-ship, was so damaged as to be obliged to leave the fleet and make for the French coast, where—in trying to go into the Seine—she ran ashore and became a total wreck. Other ships had suffered much, both in material damage and in men; and without further fighting the Armada ran on to Calais, off which they anchored on the afternoon of the 27th.

The Duke then sent a message to Parma, urging him to embark at once; but the tone of his letter implied that he expected Parma to help and protect the fleet, rather than that the fleet was prepared to ensure a safe passage to Parma. Parma's reply, which came on the 28th, was unsatisfactory. He was not ready to embark and could not be so in less than a fortnight; but even if he had been ready he could not have started till the Dutch flotilla was out of the way. If Medina Sidonia would clear the sea of Count Justin, Seymour, Howard, and all the rest of them, it would then be time to think of crossing over to England. The report of this answer and all that it implied added to the discouragement which the week's experience had impressed on the Spaniards. They had started jubilant in the expectation of a triumphant advance up the Channel and across the North Sea from the Low Countries. The reality had been one succession of disasters and of battles, in which they had suffered terribly without appearing to have inflicted any loss on their nimble assailants. And the numbers of the enemy were increasing. Many small vessels had joined the English fleet on its course up Channel; and, as Howard anchored off Calais, a gunshot to windward of the Spaniards, Seymour, with his squadron, rejoined, adding three capital ships to the fighting power. There were thus in the English fleet, of Queen's ships and merchantmen, from forty to forty-five that could be considered effective men-of-war—a fair match, so far as armament went, for the best forty or forty-five Spaniards, but in reality very superior, by reason of their mobility, steadiness, and gunnery; qualities which, though too late, the Spaniards were beginning to appreciate and fear. Their nerves were already unstrung, when, about midnight of the 28th, eight hastily improvised fire-ships came down on them with wind and tide. As they burst

into flames, Medina Sidonia made the signal to slip the cables, intending
to return in the daylight and take up his old berth. But a panic seized
the Spaniards. "The fire-ships of Antwerp!" they cried, and, cutting
their cables, they drifted away to the north. They were, for the time,
paralysed with fear. When morning came they were off Gravelines,
closely followed by the English fleet, which now attacked in its full force,
knowing that this was the crisis of the campaign. The Armada must be
driven into the North Sea, past the coast of Flanders, beyond the reach
of Parma. Seymour and Wynter, Drake, Hawkins, and Frobisher led the
several attacks; Howard, who had waited off Calais to ensure the capture
or destruction of the admiral of the galleasses, the most heavily armed
ship in the Armada, came up a little later. This galleass had injured her
rudder in the confusion of the night, and in the morning was captured
after a stubborn and hand-to-hand fight, in which her commander, Hugo
de Moncada, was killed. The French, who had not interfered during
the fight, now claimed the prize; and Howard, satisfied with her being
lost to the Spaniards, left her, and joined the main battle, which raged
fiercely during the greater part of the day.

But the superiority of the English was felt from the first, and the
want of tactical guiding was as marked in the Spanish fleet as its many
other shortcomings. The wind was at S.S.W. and the Armada had
streamed off before it. The Duke made no real effort to collect the
effective ships, many of which were far to leeward; and the brunt of the
battle fell on some fifteen which clustered round their admiral, and fought
valiantly but without avail. Of recorded incidents much might be
written; we have them in Spanish and in English, but all to the same
effect: the Spanish ships could not close with the English, and against
the English guns the Spanish guns were powerless. Some sentences from
Medina Sidonia's letter to the King put this in the clearest light. "In
the rear, Don Francisco de Toledo (in the *San Felipe*) abode the coming
of the enemy and endeavoured to grapple with them; whereupon they
assailed him, and by shooting of ordnance brought him to great
extremity. Don Diego Pimentel (in the *San Mateo*) came to relieve
him and both were hardly pressed; seeing which, Juan Martinez de
Recalde came to their assistance, with Don Augustin Mexía, and rescued
them from this strait. But notwithstanding this, these ships returned
and again assaulted the enemy; as likewise did Don Alonso de Luzon, and
the *Santa Maria de Begoña*, in which was Garibay, and the *San Juan de
Sicilia*, in which was Don Diego Tellez Enriquez. These came near to
boarding the enemy, yet could they not grapple with them; they fighting
with their great ordnance, and our men defending themselves with
harquebuss-fire and musketry, the distance being very small."

When—partly from want of ammunition, partly from hopeless
incapacity—the largest Spanish ships were reduced to answering great
guns with harquebusses, it is not surprising that the Spaniards suffered

very much, the English not at all; or that, after this terrible pounding, the *San Felipe* and the *San Mateo* tried to save themselves by running on shore on the coast of Flanders. The officers and most of the crew of the *San Felipe* escaped to Nieuport, but the ship was taken possession of by the Dutch and carried into Flushing; so also was the *San Mateo*, after a stubborn resistance which ended in the officers being taken prisoners and the men thrown overboard. Other ships went down with all hands; how many was never exactly known; so many in all were ultimately lost that the details were never fully made out. By nightfall the Spaniards were thoroughly, hopelessly beaten, and fled to the north.

*   *   *   *   *

It was then, and has ever since been, the fashion to say that England was saved from a very great danger by the providential interference of storms; to the Spaniards, it soothed the national pride; to the English, it seemed to point them out as the elect of God. In reality it was quite untrue. From the day on which the Spanish ships appeared off the Lizard till a week after the battle of Gravelines there was no wind beyond what a well-found ship would prefer; nothing to prevent frequent intercourse by small boats. Subsequently, the weather was bad, and gave effect to the damage wrought by the English guns; for the Spaniards, with no thought of Denmark or Norway, and still less of returning south, were trying to reach their own coast by passing to the west of Ireland. But they were ignorant of the navigation; they had neither pilots nor charts; their ships were not seaworthy, and the weather was wild. As they passed between the Orkney and Shetland Islands they left one ship a wreck on Fair Isle. Some were lost among the Western Hebrides; some near the Giant's Causeway and on the coast of Donegal; twelve were driven into Sligo Bay and there totally lost; others on the outer isles. "And so I can say," wrote Sir Richard Bingham, the Governor of Connaught, "by good estimation, that six or seven thousand men have been cast away on these coasts, save some thousand of them which escaped to land in several places where their ships fell, which since were all put to the sword." Others were wrecked further south. One, driven again into the Channel, was thrown ashore near Salcombe. According to the Spanish estimate, two—in addition to the *San Felipe* and *San Mateo*—were sunk in the battle, nineteen were wrecked in Scotland or Ireland, and thirty-five were not accounted for. In all, captured or destroyed, the loss of ships was returned as sixty-three, and the loss of life was in even greater proportion; for to the men of these ships who were, for the most part, drowned or butchered, must be added the very large number of those who were slain in fight, or died of wounds, sickness, cold, and famine. Few such tremendous and far-reaching catastrophes have been recorded in history.

RICHELIEU

(From volume IV, chapter IV, " Richelieu," by Stanley Leathes, M.A., formerly Fellow and Lecturer in History of Trinity College, Cambridge)

For eighteen years the great Minister had ruled the kingdom of France. He had claimed for his master and himself power over all persons and causes within the realm. He had elevated absolutism into a principle. Existing institutions, existing traditions, had been forced to give way before his will. Claiming so much, he must be brought to account for all that he claimed. His great achievements in the field of diplomacy, his personal triumphs over rivals and enemies, the creation of a French army and a French navy, the lasting impression of his overmastering personality—these things give him a great place in history. But he must also be judged by his work as an administrator, and by the effects of his work on the internal prosperity and development of France.

France needed a great administrator. The development of her institutions had not kept pace with her growth. The monarchy had accepted the heritage of a hundred feudal sovereigns; it had undertaken the task of welding a dozen races into a nation; all the men and all the treasures of the kingdom were at its disposal; the fund of loyalty and national enthusiasm on which it could draw was almost inexhaustible; but the machinery for the orderly execution of its purposes was still to be created. We may also think, and consequences were to prove, that safeguards against the abuse of its authority were needed; but we can hardly blame the statesman who saw in *Parlements* and Estates General only so many obstacles to efficiency. The materials for a constitutional monarchy may have been present in France, though they were not very obvious to view; but the materials for an orderly, law-abiding, and beneficent monarchy were certainly present, and Richelieu did little or nothing for their organisation.

*　　*　　*　　*　　*

The burden of taxation was great; the distribution of it rendered its incidence even more galling. The *pays d'états*, Languedoc, Provence, Burgundy, Britanny, paid hardly more than one-third of their proper share. Richelieu endeavoured indeed (1628–32) to assimilate the financial conditions of some of these provinces to the rest of France; but here his authority for once proved insufficient; and he had to compound with the freer provinces for the restoration of their liberties. Dauphiné alone lost its privileges. Not only did the nobles and the clergy escape the more burdensome forms of taxation; but the myriads of officials, whose numbers were constantly growing, also avoided payment. Many professions were exempt. Most of the chief towns paid a light composition for *taille*. It is estimated that a fourth of the population of France went free of direct taxation on one ground or another. Moreover, one-third of France escaped the chief part of the *gabelle*. The burden of the unprivileged and especially of the peasants was the heavier in consequence.

Richelieu himself, though profuse, was not avaricious. His income from ecclesiastical benefices was about a million and a half *livres*; and he received as much more from property and pensions. At his death his fortune, though large, was not large in proportion to his opportunities. That he himself was no financier, need not be laid to his charge. But that he did not discover and employ able financiers is largely due to the principles which governed his public action. He required his men of finance to be as subservient as his generals. His Bullions and Bouthilliers found him money; he did not understand, he did not care to understand the means. More capable ministers might have been less easy to control. Even their dishonesty was valuable, as placing them more completely in his power, should they at any time give offence.

In general administration Richelieu made little systematic improvement. Local administration, so far as it existed, was in the hands of the heads of the five-and-twenty governments into which France was divided, and of the *Parlements*. The military local authority was in the hands of the Governors, the civil authority in the hands of the *Parlements*. In times of weak government the authority of Governors had frequently been used in the cause of rebellion. Richelieu made it clear how slight that authority really was, and it was proved that the rebellion even of a Montmorency was not dangerous. But the Cardinal was naturally not inclined to increase the importance of the Governors: and their office continued to be one rather of dignity than of power. Only six months' residence was customary; and even this was frequently evaded. With the *Parlements* he was constantly in collision; they approved neither his financial edicts, nor his manner of dealing with political offenders, nor his contemptuous attitude towards the law. They were not suited for the work of administration; and, if they had been, they would not have been suited to the Cardinal. His methods were arbitrary and direct; he carried further the practice introduced by his predecessors of despatching commissioners, *maîtres des requêtes*, to districts where action was necessary; under the name of *intendants de justice, de police, et des finances*, these officers received the widest authority to override every existing functionary or institution, to order all matters at the pleasure of the central Government, to try persons and causes without regard to the formalities of law. Similar officers accompanied the armies, where their simple procedure and extensive competence proved of the highest value in controlling and regulating expenditure and supply. Eventually a system of *intendants* was created; but under Richelieu there was no system; no law prescribed the duties of *intendants* or defined their powers; the despatch of each *intendant* was an act of arbitrary force; the *intendants* were the direct agents of a lawless autocracy.

In matters relating to justice France was already well provided. The Courts of the *présidiaux* and the *Parlements*, with minor jurisdictions, covered the field well; the complaint was rather of the excessive complexity of the system and procedure, than of injustice or defect. But Richelieu made it a practice in dealing with political offenders to disregard the ordinary Courts of justice, and to proceed by the action of commissions of judges specially chosen to try the particular case. By such tribunals, Cinq-Mars, de Thou, Montmorency, the Marshal de Marillac, and many others were condemned. If a first commission showed any hesitation, it was dissolved, and a second appointed. However clear the offence, the Cardinal would not allow the law to take its normal course. The *Parlements* protested; but their protests were disregarded.

In matters relating to public order little progress was made. The nobility as a class neither required crushing, nor were crushed. Impoverished by the high rate of customary expenditure in the Court and with the army, and by the fall in the purchasing power of the fixed dues which they received from their tenants, their chief ambition was to win the favour of the Government and to secure its patronage, rather than to thwart it. The destruction of royal fortresses except on the frontier was a wise measure of economy. The destruction of the fortified residences of the nobility may or may not have been necessary as a precaution; but such residences, for the most part, were indefensible against modern ordnance, and their destruction without indemnity was in any case an injustice. The practice of the magnates to raise rebellion on any occasion of discontent required severe repression; in the process of repression it became clear how scanty were the actual resources controlled by such rebels. The general security of ordinary citizens under Richelieu's rule was neither greater nor less than it had been in earlier times, and left much to be desired. The armies, whose pay became more and more irregular, lived upon the country where they were quartered. To be treated as a conquered country implied exceptional indulgence and not the reverse. In spite of the striking example made of de Bouteville and des Chapelles, the practice of duelling was hardly less prevalent under Richelieu than it had been under Henry IV. The Cardinal's police was admirable for the discovery of secret intrigues; for the security of common people it was not intended. The almost complete freedom of the press that had existed up to 1630 was in that year destroyed; for the indulgent control of the *Parlements* and the Sorbonne was substituted a rigorous censorship: and a government permit was required for every publication. Of the press as a useful source of instruction to statesmen, he had no notion. The official *Gazette de France* contained all the information about public affairs which he thought desirable for the people.

Richelieu's friendship for letters followed the same principle as his other efforts, the establishment of a central and supreme authority. This was an age when literary and social circles or cliques exercised a considerable influence. The *dix-sept seigneurs* assembled at the house of Bassompierre, *Messieurs du Marais* in that of Madame de Rohan ; the Countess of Soissons, the Princess of Condé, held similar gatherings. The Hôtel de Rambouillet was the centre for the *précieux*. One of these clubs met at the house of Valentin Conrart to discuss literary questions. Richelieu heard of their discussions, and offered them his protection and official recognition. Though somewhat embarrassed, they had no choice but to accept, and in 1634 they were constituted as the French Academy. The *Parlement* with considerable reluctance registered their letters-patent in 1637. The number of the members from the first was forty, of whom Balzac, Voiture, Chapelain, Vaugelas were the most distinguished. They accepted their prescribed mission : to purify the French language, and to determine its canons according to the best usage. For this purpose in 1638 they began, at the suggestion of Chapelain, the compilation of their *Dictionary*, in which the influence of Vaugelas was predominant. The later history of the Academy is beyond the scope of this chapter.

The age of Richelieu was an age of a great religious revival in France. The Cardinal de Bérulle founded the Oratory, and multiplied institutions for the instruction of clergy. St Vincent de Paul founded his *Sœurs de la Charité,* and his Congregation of the Mission. The Ursulines and the Visitandines took in hand the education of girls and women. The Jesuit schoolmasters and professors were active everywhere. Richelieu himself did something for the reformation of the religious Orders, and procured his election as head of the three great Orders of Cluny, Cîteaux, and Prémontré, partly with this object. He did good service in composing the disputes between secular and regular clergy, in requiring of the religious license to preach and to confess, and in subjecting them to the authority of the Bishops. It was his ambition to become head of the Church in France, as he was ruler of the State. When the Pope thwarted his desire to be Legate for France, he dreamed of becoming Patriarch of a national Church. Yet flagrant abuses went unremedied in the Church. Non-residence, plurality of benefices, abbeys and priories in lay hands, the charging of lay pensions on ecclesiastical revenues, the employment of Cardinals and Archbishops in military commands—these disorders the Cardinal, himself a soldier and a pluralist, did not attempt to check.

He is seen perhaps at his best in his treatment of the Protestants after their pretensions to political independence had been finally suppressed. The toleration which was accorded to them was real. The greatest consideration was shown for their susceptibilities, and the hostility of the Catholic population was kept in bounds. Their pastors were exempted from *taille* ; a subvention of 200,000 *livres* was accorded to them; they were compensated for the loss of the property of the Church in Béarn. Richelieu was anxious to win over the ministers and prepare the way for a general conversion. In this he was disappointed, but individual conversions were frequent, and the Catholic clergy were taxed to provide pensions for converted Protestant ministers. Of the growing influence of Jansenist opinions he showed himself less tolerant; he inaugurated the long struggle between the monarchy and this sect by the imprisonment of the Abbé of Saint Cyran in 1638; for reasons which are not altogether clear, he saw in these opinions a danger to the State; but the time has not yet come to enlarge upon this theme.

Different estimates may be formed of the military achievements of the Cardinal; as to the general tendencies of his political action there is less room for doubt. Talents, industry, perseverance, resolution, courage, these he possessed in the highest degree. The game of politics, as he understood it and as it was generally understood, he played with consummate ability. Though at a vast expense, he checked the dangerous preponderance of the Habsburg coalition and kept for France her proper place among the Powers. That a large proportion of the sacrifices which he imposed upon his country for this end were unnecessary, that the heritage of bankruptcy which he left to his successors was due to misgovernment, that his habitual contempt of law and justice was impolitic as well as immoral, that he created no system to take the place of that which he destroyed, that the absolutism which he set up was lawless and disorderly, that he seems to have never comprehended the true bases of national prosperity and national power—these are defects which become the more flagrant the more highly we estimate his gifts. The abasement of the magnates, the suppression of the Huguenots, the Habsburg wars, even the maintenance of his personal power—these were legitimate ends. But in his choice of means he was reckless and improvident; in his choice of persons he looked for subservience rather than for independent initiative; of more exalted aims he had no conception; of mercy and justice he took no account; of creative and beneficent statesmanship he had no share. Four-fifths of the field of political endeavour he left untouched, or touched only to encumber and destroy. If the Peace of Westphalia and the Peace of the Pyrenees were of his making, so also was the Revolution of 1789. He had revealed to the French monarchy the weakness of all those traditional and conventional restraints which had limited the power of earlier Kings for good, and more especially for evil; the autocracy was slow to unlearn the lesson he had taught. The bonfires of rejoicing which celebrated his decease were premature; his death was not to ease the bondage which his living will had imposed on France.

THE LAST CAMPAIGN OF GUSTAVUS ADOLPHUS

*(From volume IV, chapter VI, " Gustavus Adolphus," by A. W. Ward,
Litt.D., F.B.A., Master of Peterhouse, Cambridge)*

But his [Gustavus'] intention of crushing the Bavarians before their
junction with Wallenstein was frustrated; though, moving on from Fürth,
he occupied the road leading from Ratisbon to Eger by Amberg and
Weiden.   The Bavarians had already reached Eger; and, massing his
forces, Wallenstein was clearly desirous of waging a decisive conflict
(June).   That, with forces scattered over so wide an area, Gustavus
should exhibit some uncertainty in his movements was inevitable; but
after he had resolved in his turn on giving battle at Nürnberg, the
energy with which he concentrated his forces is extremely remarkable.
Before the actual conflict he more than doubled his numbers, raising
them to little short of 48,000 troops, as against more than 60,000
enemies.   The latter estimate, however, is very uncertain, because of
the extraordinary numbers of non-combatants—15,000 men it is said
and as many women—comprised in Wallenstein's army.

After falling back on Nürnberg, and marking out a camp for his
forces on the western and southern sides of the city, Gustavus paused to
await both the arrival of the enemy and that of his own reinforcements.
The fortifications of Nürnberg itself were strengthened, and the citizens
cheerfully prepared for the defence, contrasting—if we may attach
credit to a song of the day—their own hopefulness, as they beheld
their " father " and his " heroes " in their midst, with the desolation of
Magdeburg when her fate was upon her.   By the middle of the month
Wallenstein had taken up his position in a vast fortified camp which
extended on the left bank of the Regnitz as far as Fürth immediately
opposite Nürnberg, and faced the main Swedish position from heights
covered with batteries.   The Swedes had failed in all their attempts to
prevent the construction of the vast camp which threatened an effective
blockade of the city and of the Swedish camp at its gates.   Within
the walls the signs of famine were already at hand; for the town was
crowded with fugitive peasantry; and the ravages of disease were
spreading among the Swedish soldiery.

Soon after the middle of August, however, Gustavus had gathered
his forces, Wallenstein, strangely as it was thought, hazarding no interference with the arrival of the service contingents.   The most important
of these was that brought by Oxenstierna from Rhine and Mosel, with
which, after effecting a junction with the troops of Banér and those of
William of Weimar, he had reached Nürnberg on August 20.   All was
now ready for a decisive struggle.

On August 31, the Swedish army was drawn up in fighting order along the Regnitz opposite Wallenstein's camp. But he would not accept battle. A cannonade opened on the following day remained ineffectual; and on the night of September 2 the Swedes crossed the Regnitz at a lower point, and pitched their camp immediately opposite that of the enemy. On the morning of the 3rd the attack upon the heights on the northern side of the camp began. The chief point of attack and defence was the *alte Veste*, a ruined castle in the middle of a clearance of the wood which had been specially fortified by the Wallensteiners; thrice the Swedes entered it, and thrice they were ejected from its walls. The struggle continued *caldissimamente*, in Wallenstein's phrase, till darkness and the fall of rain rendered its continuance on the part of the Swedes impossible. But they held their ground during the night, and in the morning essayed another attack, but again in vain. Hereupon Gustavus withdrew his troops into the camp at Fürth.

The King frankly confessed to the Nürnbergers the failure of his great effort, but the preparations in which he engaged for constructing another camp showed that he had as yet no design of moving. Hereupon he once more tried negotiations with the adversary whose resistance had at last stayed his victorious course. The intermediary was the Imperialist general Sparre, one of Wallenstein's former agents, who had been taken prisoner by the Swedes. Thurn, too, and the Bohemian agitator Bubna were in the King's camp, and may have contributed to complicate the situation. But the proposals of Gustavus, placed on record by Oxenstierna, were both clear and moderate. Pomerania and the dignity of a Prince of the Empire were to be the King's own "satisfaction"; the Elector Palatine was to be restored, but so likewise was the Elector of Mainz; Saxony and Brandenburg were to be compensated by Magdeburg and Halberstadt; Wallenstein by a duchy of Franconia. The Emperor was to guarantee these arrangements. But Gustavus' offer of a conference on the question of peace, to be held in the sight of both armies, was declined by Wallenstein till he should have referred the proposal to the Emperor. (It was actually referred to him, and an indecisive answer came two months afterwards.) As we know from Oxenstierna, the impression left on Gustavus by the apathetic bearing of Wallenstein was that no settlement remained possible between them but war to the knife.

Meanwhile, though Gustavus had pressed forward the entrenchments, the lack of provisions was becoming serious on his side; and Wallenstein was in his turn being pressed by those around him to assume the offensive. But he was still immovable. At last the King, in order if possible to "draw the fox," resolved on abandoning his position. Placing a garrison of nearly 5000 in Nürnberg, and sending a formal challenge of battle for the morrow to Wallenstein, he broke up his camp on September 18. Three days later, after the Swedes had reached Neustadt (near Coburg),

Wallenstein also broke up his camp, and, burning down the villages round Nürnberg, marched north.

The course now pursued by Gustavus Adolphus is open to much criticism; nor can it be denied that his wonderful versatility and buoyancy at this time began to resemble a hazardous mutability of design. It should, however, be noted that the plan on which he now resolved had the persistent approval of Oxenstierna, who so often, as he told the King, had occasion to pour water upon his fire. Gustavus determined on returning to Swabia, and thence, moving down the Danube, to invade the Austrian lands, where he reckoned on being supported by a rising among the sturdy peasants of Upper Austria, of whose continued unrest satisfactory assurances had reached him. Wallenstein, the King seems to have calculated, would by such a movement be drawn out of Saxony; and in the meantime he ordered a Swedish force under Duwall from the Brandenburg side to join Arnim, who now had 16,000 men under his command. If, however, it proved necessary to furnish Saxony with further assistance, this task was to fall to Bernard of Weimar, who was placed at the head of the force in Franconia during the illness of his elder brother, William. Yet, when Bernard proposed to move forward on his own account, the King showed much displeasure. He had once more modified or postponed his plan of action; and after crossing the Danube at Donauwörth, and recapturing Rain, halted at Neuburg, with the intention of continuing his march to the Lake of Constance (October). Here at last definite news reached him of Wallenstein's movements, and an interval of high-strung expectation ended in clear and firm resolve.

Notwithstanding the doubts of Gustavus, who remembered the old dealings with Arnim and his master, Wallenstein had never hesitated in his determination to crush the Saxons, after Gustavus had himself failed to come to their aid. Against Arnim, Maradas had led an Imperialist force from Bohemia; and, in the middle of August, Field-Marshal Holk had by Wallenstein's orders broken into the south-west of the Electorate, and finally carried his raids as far as the neighbourhood of Dresden. Holk, a Dane and a Lutheran by birth and breeding, who had formerly served against Wallenstein at Stralsund, by the brutal excesses of his flying column earned for himself in the Erzgebirge and its near neighbourhood a long-enduring infamy. In September Wallenstein detached Gallas with a force of from 10,000 to 12,000 in Holk's wake; and, in the middle of October, the Bavarian troops having marched south to operate nearer home against the Swedes, himself approached by way of Thuringia, and after effecting a junction with both Holk and Gallas, reached Leipzig. Both town and castle (the Pleissenburg) after a show of resistance capitulated. The Commander-in-Chief was here also joined by Aldringer, with a division from Bavaria, and by Pappenheim, who during the greater part of the year had been carrying on successful operations in the north-west against the Swedish commanders Tott and Baudissin, and against the wary Duke George of Lüneburg. With some reluctance Pappenheim relinquished a kind of warfare in which he excelled, and took up his position, near that of Wallenstein, at Halle. The whole district between the Elbe and Saale was now under the control of the Imperialists, whose head-quarters were at Weissenfels. Their entire force (including the Pappenheimers) may be reckoned at over 25,000 foot and 15,000 horse, with, it is stated, 70 guns. But, as in the case of the Swedish army, there is much uncertainty in this estimate.

Sure at last of Wallenstein's purpose, Gustavus determined upon keeping his promise to the Saxon Elector. The intentions of John George may even now have seemed doubtful to the King; but whether Wallenstein were to crush Saxony, or whether it were to lapse into neutrality, Gustavus, as he seems now to have fully recognised, would be placed in an impossible position. His way home would be blocked, his tenure of Pomerania imperilled by the "Duke of Mecklenburg," and the freedom of the Baltic might once more be threatened by the Imperial Commander-in-Chief. If so, where was he to look for allies? Denmark's jealousy was stronger than ever. The desire of the United Provinces for peace grew with the revived ambition of Spain to take part in the war. He could place no trust in English diplomacy, which in the person of Sir Henry Vane continued to occupy itself with the subsidiary question of the restoration of Charles I's brother-in-law. Even France, while leaving the subsidies promised at Bärwalde unpaid, was alike intent upon her own operations on the Rhine, and undesirous of making Gustavus the arbiter of the German War. His progress had reached a stage of great difficulty, and we know for certain that in these closing weeks of his career of conquest his mind was much occupied with what had been his primary concern when he had opened his German campaigns—the problems of safeguarding the destinies of his own Swedish kingdom.

On October 17 the Swedish army reached Nördlingen; and on the 24th Gustavus rode into the faithful city of Nürnberg, there to confer with Oxenstierna on the situation. The Chancellor was to remain as the King's plenipotentiary in southern Germany, with instructions to summon to Ulm a meeting of the Swabian, Franconian, and two Rhenish Circles, which should there renounce their allegiance to the Emperor, accept the King's "direction and protection," and order a general excise towards the prosecution of the war. The Chancellor received the King's instructions as to the government of his daughter and heiress, Christina, should his death take place during her minority. At Erfurt Gustavus bade farewell to his Queen, and on November 11 he reached Naumburg, about nine miles from Weissenfels. After the Hessians and the Weimarers had joined him, his force is reckoned to have amounted to 19,000 foot, with 6500 horse and 60 guns.

The troops of John George of Saxony and Duke George of Lüneburg were not on the spot. Arnim, who commanded the Saxon forces that were still in Silesia, was busily negotiating according to his wont. But with all his coming and going, Gustavus' urgent entreaties could not induce the Elector to do more than order two regiments of horse to march south with the Lüneburg troops. None of these, or of the Saxons, appeared on the field of battle.

To keep in touch with Pappenheim, Wallenstein moved back his main army on Merseburg and Lützen, and by this movement induced Gustavus to advance. On the evening of November 15 the Swedes stood on the border of the great plain which opens east of the Saale upon Lützen, Markranstädt, and Leipzig—in this war, as in the Napoleonic, the chosen battle-field of the nations. On the morning of the 16th, in a November fog, the battle of Lützen began. The high road to Leipzig had been entrenched by Wallenstein and was defended by artillery. Behind it stood his army, in three lines of battle, with cavalry on either wing; upon it the Swedes advanced in their lighter formation of two lines, the King and his blue and yellow guards on the right; Bernard of Weimar (but as to this the accounts differ) in command on the left. About ten o'clock the fog for a time dispersed, and the attack, led by the King in person, began. Notwithstanding a charge of Ottavio Piccolomini's cavalry, the Swedes had taken the battery on the road, but they were driven out again; and, as the fog thickened, Gustavus, hastening to the assistance of one of his regiments, was momentarily isolated and carried among the enemy's cavalry. His horse received a wound, and then he was wounded himself, whereupon he begged the Duke Francis Albert of Lauenburg to help him from the field; but the Duke fled. A royal page (Leubelfing) remained by the side of his master, when some troopers rode up and put an end to his life. His body was found naked, and covered with wounds. The supposed foul play on the part of the Duke of Lauenburg is an exploded fiction.

This happened about noon. But the battle continued to rage till nightfall. So soon as the King's death became known the command of his army was taken over by Bernard of Weimar. Pappenheim, whose cavalry now intervened in the battle, was in his turn mortally wounded; he died next day at Leipzig. After the Imperialists had recovered their batteries on the high road, they were finally driven out by the valour of the Swedish infantry; but nearly the whole of the Yellow Regiment was destroyed in the process. Late in the evening, after making a last attempt to rally his yielding troops, Wallenstein ordered retreat to be sounded, and Leipzig was reached in the course of the night. He had left 6000 dead on the field, the Swedes 4000. The stern judgment afterwards held by Wallenstein at Prague, when he magisterially distributed capital and other punishments as well as large pecuniary rewards, seems to indicate that he had no choice but to retreat. Yet though the Swedes held their ground, they ventured on no pursuit. Both sides thought fit to claim the victory, and a *Te Deum* was celebrated at Vienna. The exultation, however, both here and at Madrid, where the *Death of the King of Sweden* was enacted on a stage accustomed to present to its spectators miracles and visitations of divine Providence, was due to a single incident in the battle, rather than to its general result.

The death of Gustavus Adolphus, at the height of his fame and almost at the height of his power—when still in the prime of life (he was not yet thirty-nine years of age) and full of aspirations which, marvellous as his career had been, were still unsatisfied—struck the world with awe, and was fitly moralised by Cardinal Richelieu, the man who best knew how to turn the event to political account. The full significance of the removal of such a personality from the very midst of the scene of military as well as that of political action it would be almost impossible to overestimate. He was great, not only because of what he achieved, but of what he set himself to accomplish. Oxenstierna may have been warranted in asserting that his master intended to be Emperor of Scandinavia, and to rule over an empire comprising all the Baltic lands. He certainly meant Sweden to be made impregnably strong, and left free to hold to the faith which she had chosen. Thus, as the simple triplet on the stone at Breitenfeld avers, he saved religious liberty for the world. He did so consciously, and not as a mere consequence of his political designs. To the fulfilment of his purpose he brought the gifts of a born ruler of men, as well as those of a great general and a great statesman. Cast in heroic mould, of commanding stature and fair-haired (*re d'oro*), he was a Swede every inch of him. Affable, free of speech, full of wrath if discipline were broken or disaster provoked, he was the comrade of his soldiers, by whose side he fought and prayed. He was at the same time a master of military detail; his reforms were grounded on experience, and his tactics inspired by the prescience of victory. He had been carefully trained in the art of government, and besides being able to speak eight languages, and interested in letters and learning, was versed in the administrative business of his own country and capable of understanding the political systems of other lands. He was an adept in negotiation; he was proof against the diplomatic insinuations of Wallenstein, and met as an equal the statecraft of Richelieu. His occasional political miscalculations and his strategic mistakes—not always easily distinguishable from one another—were almost invariably redeemed by his courage and resource; but the foundation of his strength lay in his unfaltering conviction that his cause was that of his country and one of which God had charged him with the defence.

THE IMPEACHMENT OF STRAFFORD

(From volume IV, chapter IX, "The First Two Years of the Long Parliament," by G. W. Prothero, Litt.D., F.B.A., Hon. and Late Fellow and Tutor of King's College, Cambridge)

WHEN the great assembly which was afterwards to be known as the Long Parliament met at Westminster on November 3, 1640, the condition of affairs was very different from what it had been in the spring of the year. It was plain, even to the King, that concessions must now be made. The Crown would probably have to surrender the claim to levy ship-money, and even the customs duties, without consent of Parliament, to abolish monopolies, and to extend the limits of religious toleration; but subsequent events showed that Charles had no intention of seriously modifying the ecclesiastical system, of accepting the principle of ministerial responsibility, or of binding himself to summon Parliaments regularly; in other words, he clung to the essentials of prerogative. The parliamentary leaders, on their part, while resolved to carry out the programme which Pym had indicated in the previous April, had at first no intention of pushing matters to extremes. Their aim was rather restorative—their plan, to thrust back the encroaching power of the Crown, to sweep away the bulwarks of despotism, to revive ancient rights and safeguards. But, as is usual in revolutionary times, mutual suspicion and mistrust prevented a halt when the work of restoration was complete; and it was at this point that the vacillating and shifty character of Charles proved of so fatal a significance. The conviction became ineradicable that the King intended, at the earliest opportunity, to withdraw the concessions into which he had been forced; and it must be allowed that, so early as the summer of 1641, incidents, to be noted later, occurred which lent only too much colour to this suspicion. Thus the measures promoted by Parliament, in order to safeguard the rights which had been gained, became more and more subversive of the old order, while acts of violence on the King's part betrayed more and more hostility towards the parliamentary party; and the two sides were gradually driven into a position of antagonism, of which the only outcome could be civil war.

The most important event of the first six months of the Long Parliament was undoubtedly the trial of Strafford, which led to his execution on May 12, 1641. So long as influences hostile to reform surrounded the King, so long as the executive remained in the hands of men not only independent of, but hostile to, parliamentary control, a reconciliation between the Crown and the nation would be impossible. It was therefore upon the instruments of autocracy that Pym and his colleagues concentrated their attention. Abandoning the lengthy method hitherto followed, of investigating and expounding grievances, they resolved to strike boldly at the root of the mischief. Within a few days of the meeting of Parliament, a list of persons to be impeached was drawn up; it included, among others, the names of Strafford and Laud. The parliamentary leaders were not, however, in any hurry for the attack; they intended to begin by collecting evidence and making sure of their ground. That the plan was altered, and the first blow struck swiftly, was due to the fact that Strafford, hearing of their intention and anxious to anticipate his accusers, urged the King to charge Pym and others with treason, on account of their dealings with the Scots. The King hesitated; and the opportunity was lost. Pym, who was throughout remarkably well informed as to the intentions of the Court, at once carried the impeachment to the Lords; and on November 11 Strafford was committed to prison.

The importance of this initial success was very great; for it not only removed from the King's side his most devoted supporter, a counsellor whose advice would at least have been clear and energetic, but it struck terror into the hearts of others connected with the system which Strafford had upheld. It showed, moreover, that the Lords were ready to support their colleagues in the Lower House, who were therefore emboldened to proceed. The blow was speedily followed up. An attack on the relaxation of the penal laws caused (December 10) the flight of Secretary Windebank, known to have been in close touch with Panzani, and suspected of being himself a Catholic. A resolution, declaring that ship-money was illegal, and that the Judges who decided against Hampden had broken the law, led to the flight of Lord Keeper Finch (December 21). He was promptly impeached. In the following February, Judge Berkeley, whose support of the Crown had been peculiarly outspoken, was summoned from the Bench itself before the bar of the House, and committed to custody. The assumption by Convocation, in the previous summer, of rights independent of Parliament had aroused much feeling; and the canons which it had passed were condemned on political and religious grounds. These were now declared to be illegal; and Laud was impeached of high treason (December 18). Articles against him were voted in February; and on March 1 he was sent to the Tower. Thus all the most important agents of the monarchy were swept away.

Meanwhile the charges against Strafford had been roughly formulated (November 24). Several of these, such as the statements that he had maliciously stirred up strife between England and Scotland, and had embezzled public money, were exaggerated or absurd; what was serious and, indeed, undeniable, was the twofold charge that he had "endeavoured to subvert the fundamental laws and government of England and Ireland, and instead thereof to introduce an arbitrary and tyrannical government against law," and that "he had laboured to subvert the rights of Parliaments and the ancient course of parliamentary proceedings." Evidence in support of these accusations was actively collected during the next two months; and the detailed Articles were voted on January 30, 1641. Three weeks later, Strafford put in his answer before the Lords; and Charles gave grievous offence by being present on the occasion, and making no secret of his satisfaction with Strafford's defence. The Peers voted that all that had been done in his presence was null and void; nevertheless, they allowed Strafford another month to prepare his case. The impatience and irritation of the Commons grew day by day. Although many important steps (presently to be noticed) had already been taken towards re-establishing the authority of Parliament, nothing, it was evident, could be regarded as secure till the main issue had been tried and settled in the case of the chief adviser of the Crown.

On March 22, 1641, the great trial began. It was a memorable scene. In that ancient hall, the work of the most tyrannical of the Norman Kings, the policy of one of the most despotic of his successors was arraigned, before a Court consisting of all the highest in the land, by the representatives of the nation which he had sought to bind. The ultimate issues went far beyond the immediate result for the individual primarily concerned. Two conceptions of government were brought face to face—government by prerogative alone, and government by King and Parliament. Pym had declared Parliament to be " the soul of the body politic"; Charles and Strafford had deliberately attempted to eliminate it from the Constitution. In the trial of Strafford this issue came to a head. The chief obstacles to the success of Pym and his colleagues lay in the difficulty of bringing Strafford's action within the legal conception of treason. Pym refused to restrict it, as heretofore, to attacks upon the person or authority of the sovereign; in his mind, an attack upon the Constitution was the more heinous crime. He sought to combine the two ideas by showing that an attempt to undermine the laws on which the authority of the monarchy reposed was to attack the sovereign in his political capacity and to threaten him with ruin. But this was a subtle and a novel idea, involving a new interpretation of the law; and, had the King frankly allowed the trial to take its course, it is at least possible that Strafford might have obtained an acquittal. But this was not to be. The army in the north was getting out of hand, and became more and more irritated with Parliament, which it regarded as the cause of its receiving no pay. This was, in a sense, true; for Parliament could not pay off the English army without also paying off and disbanding the Scots; and to disband the Scots was to deprive Parliament of its best allies. A petition was promoted among the officers, which was to be sent to the King, assuring him of their support against pressure on the part of Parliament. Two courtiers, Sir John Suckling and Henry Jermyn, with the connivance of the Queen, endeavoured to utilise this state of feeling in the concoction of a plot for transferring the command of the army to Colonel George Goring, and in some way or other—the details remained undetermined—bringing armed force to bear on the political problem. But differences of opinion arose; and Goring, in a fit of personal pique, divulged the plot.

Pym now made up his mind that Strafford must be brought to the block. Had the parliamentary party been able to trust the King, extreme measures would have been unnecessary; but the Army Plot deepened the distrust already felt, and convinced Pym and others that death was the only security against Strafford's being employed again. The charge of advising the King to bring in the Irish army was now actively pressed. Strafford, ill as he was, defended himself with marvellous skill and courage. Reminding his judges that the evidence of a single witness (Sir Henry Vane) was insufficient to prove a charge of treason, he denied that he had ever intended that the Irish army should land in England, but asserted that "in case of absolute necessity...when all other ordinary means fail," the King may "employ the best and uttermost of his means for the preserving of himself and his people." The defence made a favourable impression; and, as the trial went on, it gradually became clear that an acquittal on the charge of treason was probable. The King had been requested by both Houses to disband the Irish army from which so much was feared; it told against the prisoner that Charles for some time sent no reply, and eventually refused to disband the army till the present business should be over. Nevertheless, on April 10, the friction between the two Houses was such that the trial was temporarily adjourned. A few days later, the "inflexible party" in the Commons decided on a radical alteration in the method of attack, and brought in a Bill of Attainder—in other words, a *privilegium* to meet the special case, in lieu of a trial by impeachment under the ordinary law. The Lords, indignant, declared that the trial must proceed. The Commons were divided on the question; Pym and Hampden advised the continuation of the trial. But on April 19 the Lower House voted by a majority of three to one that Strafford's acts amounted to treason; henceforward the Bill was inevitable, and it was read a third time by 204 votes to 59. The 59 "Straffordians" were the germ of the later Royalist party; a comparison between this vote and that on the Grand Remonstrance gives a measure of the strength conferred upon that party by the subsequent religious quarrel.

While the Attainder Bill was under discussion in the Upper House, Charles made efforts to conciliate the parliamentary leaders. It was rumoured that they were to be given high office; Pym had more than one interview with the King. On the other hand, intrigues with the army went on; preparations were made for enabling Strafford to escape; an attempt, by Charles' orders, to introduce an armed force, under Captain Billingsley, into the Tower, failed and was discovered. The betrothal of the Princess Mary to Prince William of Orange (May 2, 1641), in itself a welcome event, could not allay the growing alarm and irritation.

It was this dread of military violence that, more than anything else, determined Strafford's fate, as it was afterwards to prove the immediate cause of the Civil War.   Under its influence a strongly-worded protestation was drawn up in the Lower House, binding those who signed it to defend "with life, power, and estate, the true reformed Protestant religion," the King's "person, honour, and estate," "the power and privileges of Parliament," and "the lawful rights and liberties of subjects."   This pledge, a sort of English "Covenant," was adopted, not only by the Commons, but by all the Protestant Lords, and eagerly taken up in the City.   The timely disclosure by Pym of Goring's plot and other military intrigues (May 5) intensified the prevailing anxiety, and finally brought over the Upper House.   Essex had, a week before, spoken the grim words, "Stone-dead hath no fellow"; and the bulk of the Peers were now of the same mind.   A Bill prohibiting the dissolution of Parliament without its own consent was hurried through the Lower House, and proceeded *pari passu* with the Bill of Attainder in the House of Lords.   The Lords wished to limit the duration of the anti-dissolution Bill to two years—a wise provision; but the Commons refused, and the Lords gave way.   Both Bills were read a third time on May 8.   The London mob paraded the streets, raged about Whitehall, and clamoured for execution.   After two days of agonising doubt and hesitation, the King gave his assent to both Bills; and on May 12 Strafford met his death with dignity and courage on Tower Hill.

THE OVERTHROW OF THE FRENCH DIRECTORY

(From volume VIII, chapter XXII, " Brumaire," by
H. A. L. Fisher, M.A., Fellow and Tutor of New College, Oxford)

It was now past five; and, as the legislators of the last revolutionary Assembly of France were pursuing their devious flight through the park under the opaque mist of a November evening, and leaving shreds of their crimson robes on the orange trees, Lucien, whose readiness and melodramatic gift never failed him through the day, hurried to the *Anciens* to explain the situation. With calculated pathos he depicted the affray in the Lower Chamber, the daggers drawn on Bonaparte, and the conspiracy against the Republic. Quickened and encouraged by this intelligence, Cornudet's commission proceeded to draft the required decree, which named Bonaparte, Sieyès, and Ducos provisional Consuls, adjourned the Councils till February 20, and created an intermediary Legislative Commission formed from the *Anciens*, who acted upon the assumption that the other Council had dissolved itself. Between 7 and 8 p.m. the decree was passed with one dissentient voice, and the *Anciens* adjourned till 9. During the interval a remnant of the fugitive Five Hundred, varying according to different accounts from twenty-four to a hundred and fifty, were being gathered together by the emissaries of Lucien and called to the Orangerie. It was seen that the concurrence of the Second Chamber would give constitutional authority to the acts of the conspirators; and, when the Rump opened its sittings at nine o'clock in the dim light of three candles, all the formalities were observed. Lucien took the chair; Chazal proposed a motion, which differed merely from the decree which had passed the *Anciens* in respect of the composition of the Legislative Commission, which was now to be derived from both Councils; and a committee was appointed to present a report. In the interval of its deliberations a vote was passed that Lefebvre, Murat, and Gardanne, with the soldiers who had acted under their command, had deserved well of their country; and Lucien improved the weary hours of the night by a third oration upon the legendary daggers, which formed the official apology for the use of force, and the resort to constitutional revision.

At 11 o'clock the Committee returned and presented its propositions. The Directory was to be abolished, and the provisional government entrusted to Bonaparte, Sieyès, and Ducos. The Legislature was adjourned till February 20, 1800, but 62 members of the opposition were excluded from it by name, and a commission of 25 members was appointed to act in conjunction with the commission of the *Anciens* in all urgent matters of police, legislation, and finance, to prepare necessary organic changes, and to elaborate a civil code. At 1 a.m. the measure passed the *Anciens*; and an hour later the three Consuls were summoned to the Orangerie to swear "fidelity to the Republic one and indivisible, to liberty, equality, and the representative system." Vague words denoted vague aspirations, but the dominant thought of the Revisionists was aptly rendered by Boulay when in moving the resolutions in the Orangerie he spoke of nationalising the Republic. At 3 a.m. Bonaparte drove back to Paris with Sieyès and Lucien, silent and wrapped in thought. It was 4.30 a.m. before the *Anciens* had named their commission; and the first streak of dawn must have been shining in the sky before the last of the legislators recrossed the barriers. Paris was calm and satisfied with the event. The story of the daggers had been announced at the theatres by the agents of Fouché on the night before; and in the morning the citizens of the capital read upon the posters how twenty assassins had attacked General Bonaparte in the Council of Five Hundred, and how his life had been saved by the brave grenadiers of the Legislature. Two days later the *Moniteur* recounted that Thomas Thomé, the grenadier, whose sleeve had been torn in defending Bonaparte from the blow of a dagger, had breakfasted and dined with the general, and that *la citoyenne* Bonaparte had embraced Thomas Thomé and put upon his finger a diamond ring valued at two thousand crowns.

De Tocqueville has said of the *coup d'état* of Brumaire that nothing could have been worse conceived or worse conducted. Yet it accomplished its object without the shedding of a drop of blood; and, as the Prussian ambassador in Paris pointed out to his master, it differed from all previous revolutionary days, in that it brought neither suspicion nor fear, but rather universal joy and hope. A member of the *Anciens* reflected the general feeling, when he told his constituents that it was not a case of one faction vanquishing another; that it was the Republic which had triumphed over the agitators, the French people who had triumphed over anarchy and royalism. The country was well content that the "lawyers' clerks" should return to their office-stools, and cease their sterile discordant clamours. France was tired of the revolutionary phraseology and the revolutionary legislation, of the oft-repeated formulae which had cloaked tenuity of thought, and of the feverish rush of decrees which had perpetuated discord and perplexed administration. The whole country was content to subscribe to the dictum of that deputy of the Meuse, who, in apologising for the *coup d'état* to his Department, said that of all the curses which can afflict the moral world there is none more terrible than the permanence of a body which ceaselessly deliberates and ceaselessly makes laws. Those who lived through the period which elapsed between 18 Fructidor and 18 Brumaire never forgot their sensations of impotence and despair. It seemed that the Terror had become a chronic malady, and that the virus of civil strife was too deeply set in the body politic to be eliminated even by heroic remedies. It was a Terror without the consolations of hope, unredeemed by great achievements, and leading to no salutary end. But in the hour of darkness Bonaparte returned, a brilliant ray shooting from the mysterious East, and the ugly shadows melted suddenly away. Here was the man raised above the ignoble strife of parties, the man of firm will, clear eye, and abrupt speech, who would clinch the Revolution and reconcile liberty with order. Men of every type concurred in his enterprise, aiding it either with secret prayers or overt act: soldiers from the Army of the Rhine, soldiers from the Army of Italy, men of the Mountain and men of the Plain, doctrinaires of the Institute who denied God, doctrinaires of royalism who affirmed the Tridentine decrees, peasants whose sole passion was for their plot of land, burgesses who cared for little but a quiet life, bankers who craved for enlarged credit, diplomats who wished to see amenity restored to public life, all who cared for peace, all who cared for social stability, all who cared for the glory of France. Little sympathy was felt for the fallen Councils. They had talked wildly and governed ill. They had not even made the long expected Civil Code, or cured the desperate finance which had brought the monarchy to its grave. In the government of the Directors France had discovered neither virtue, intellect, nor wisdom. To be a Director of the French Republic was indeed, as Sieyès said, a trade above all others "terrible and infernal." Yet though much was to be gained by the concentration of the executive authority, and much also by the suppression of extravagant political debate, the price was destined to be such as no one in France imagined on that November evening, while the deputies were rushing wildly through the park, and the fog was falling upon the last fevers of the French Revolution.

NAPOLEON AT ST HELENA

(From volume IX, chapter XXIV, "St Helena," by
H. A. L. Fisher, M.A., Fellow and Tutor of New College, Oxford)

THE abdication of Napoleon, his retirement from Paris to Malmaison, and his flight to Rochefort, have been related in a previous chapter. When Napoleon arrived at that port (July 3, 1815), he found the coast narrowly watched by British sail, and hazard upon every side. For ten days he waited to balance chances, conscious of a certain loss of elasticity in himself, listening to the counsels of others, himself indifferent. A clandestine escape, an ignominious capture in the ballast of a Danish sloop or in an open row-boat, would have been inconsistent with an impressive close; and, after some hesitation, he rejected all desperate expedients and determined to throw himself on the generosity of the English people. On July 13 he wrote to the Prince Regent that he had terminated his political career, and that he came, like Themistocles, to seat himself at the hearth of the British nation and to claim the protection of her laws. Two days later he gave himself into the charge of Captain Maitland of the *Bellerophon.* He knew well that he could expect little mercy from the restored Government of France, and that the Prussians would shoot him like a dog. But England was the refuge of the homeless and the asylum of the exile. She had sheltered Paoli, the friend of his youth; she had sheltered the Bourbons, the rivals of his manhood. Out of magnanimity she might shelter him.

But the man whose ambition had wrought such disasters could not expect to be treated with leniency; and the British Government determined that Napoleon was no guest, but a prisoner of war. It was a case of policy, not of precedents; and, even if Lord Liverpool's Cabinet had been accessible to quixotic impulses, it would have been their plain duty to suppress them in the interests of European peace. The Congress of Vienna had declared Napoleon to be an outlaw, and, in virtue of a Convention struck on August 2, 1815, the four Great Powers agreed to regard him as their common prisoner. The turn of events had devolved upon Great Britain the ungracious office of the gaoler; but Austria, Russia, and Prussia were consenting parties; and all four Powers promised to name commissioners to assure themselves of Napoleon's presence in the place of his captivity. Meanwhile, on July 28, the British Government had decided to send their captive to St Helena. In that lonely island of the Atlantic, with its precipitous coast, its scanty harbourage, its sparse population, the great prisoner of state might be securely guarded, the more so as the East India Company, to whom the island belonged, had recently erected upon it a complete system of semaphores. The climate was reported to be salubrious; and in St Helena Napoleon might enjoy a larger measure of liberty than any government would then have been prepared to concede to him in Europe. It was a hard fate, but brighter than an Austrian fortress, and gentler than the doom of Murat and of Ney.

On August 7 he was removed to H.M.S. *Northumberland*, which, under the command of Admiral Sir George Cockburn, was instructed to convey him to his destination. His suite consisted of twenty-five persons, including Count Montholon and General Gourgaud, who had served as adjutants in the last campaign; General Bertrand, who had controlled his household in Elba; Count de Las Cases, once a royal *émigré*, now one of the most attached of his adherents; and Dr Barry O'Meara, the surgeon of the *Bellerophon*, who, at Napoleon's request and with the consent of the British Government, was allowed to act as his medical attendant. Montholon and Bertrand were accompanied by their wives, Las Cases by his son. On October 17, at the hour of eight in the evening, after a passage of ninety-five days, Napoleon landed at Jamestown. As the house destined for his reception was not yet ready, he took up his residence at the Briars, a villa belonging to a merchant named Balecombe, where he spent some weeks in pleasant and familiar intercourse with the family of his host. In December the exiles moved into Longwood, a low wooden building on the wind-swept plateau, far above the prying curiosity of the port. It was here that the last scene in Napoleon's life-drama was enacted.

For the general history of Europe the captivity at St Helena possesses a double interest. Not only did it invest the career of the fallen hero with an atmosphere of martyrdom and pathos which gave to it a new and distinct appeal, but it enabled him to arrange a pose before the mirror of history, to soften away all that had been ungracious and hard and violent, and to draw in firm and authoritative outline a picture of his splendid achievements and liberal designs. The Napoleonic legend has been a force in the politics of Europe; and the legend owes much to the artifice of the exiles. The great captain, hero of adventures wondrous as the Arabian Nights, passes over the mysterious ocean to his lonely island and emerges transfigured as in some ennobling mirage. He shares the agonies of Prometheus, benefactor of humanity, chained to his solitary rock; his spirit is with Marcus Aurelius, moving in the serene orbit of humane and beneficent wisdom. The seed sown from St Helena fell upon fruitful soil and was tended by devout hands.

Carrel, the great Liberal journalist of the July monarchy, claims Napoleon, on the ground of the Longwood conversations, as the friend of the Republic which he overturned. Quinet sings of him as of some vague and romantic embodiment of the democratic spirit:

> "*J'ai couronné le peuple en France, en Allemagne;*
> *Je l'ai fait gentilhomme autant que Charlemagne;*
> *J'ai donné des aïeux à la foule sans nom;*
> *Des nations partout j'ai gravé le blason.*"

The heir of the Napoleonic House, Louis Bonaparte, son of the ex-King of Holland, knew well how to exploit the democratic elements in his uncle's career. In 1831 he was secretly negotiating with Republican leaders in Paris; in 1832 he published a statement in his *Rêveries politiques* that his principles were "entirely republican." In 1839 a slender volume came from the same pen, entitled *Idées Napoléoniennes*, which contained the whole essence of the exilic literature and the whole programme of the liberal Empire. The *Siècle*, a Bonapartist organ, spoke in 1840 of "the sublime agony of St Helena, longer than the agony of Christ, and no less resigned"; and in the haze of sentiment men lost sight of the elementary facts of Napoleon's career. "The thought of Napoleon at St Helena," say the editors of the official *Correspondance* (vol. xxix), "is a thought of emancipation for humanity, of democratic progress, of the application of the great principles of the Revolution"; and this was the pretext and apology for the Second Empire, the Government which, beginning with a cannonade in the Boulevards, ended with the capitulation of Sedan and the loss of Alsace and Lorraine.

Exile is in itself a form of martyrdom; and the exiles of Longwood ate their bread in genuine sorrow. As Las Cases remarked, "The details of St Helena are unimportant; to be there at all is the great grievance." A little company of French gentlemen and ladies, accustomed to the stirring life of a brilliant capital, found itself pitched on a desolate island, far from friends and home and all the great movement of the world. The attendants of Napoleon were not cast in the stoical mould; and, even if considerations of policy had not been involved, temperament would have inclined them to exaggerate minor discomforts, to strain against the restrictions of the governor, to shudder at the rocks and ravines, to condemn the rain when it was rainy, the sun when it was sunny, and the wind when it was windy, to compare the sparse gum-trees of the Longwood plateau with the ample shades of Marly and St Cloud, and the rough accommodation of the Longwood house with the comforts of a well-appointed Parisian hotel. To a man like Napoleon, whose whole soul was in politics, seclusion was a kind of torture. He had no administrative occupations to absorb his energies as had been the case in Elba; and "time," to quote his own bitter phrase, was now "his only superfluity." To quicken all the leaden hours was a task too heavy even for his busy genius. He learnt a little English, he dictated memoirs, he played chess, he read books and newspapers, he set Gourgaud mathematical problems, and in the later half of 1819 and the earlier half of 1820 he found some solace in gardening. In the first two years of his captivity his spirits were sometimes high and even exuberant; and in the exercise of his splendid intellect he must have found some genuine enjoyment. But at heart he was miserable, spiting himself like a cross child, and allowing petty insults to fester within him. Now he was calm, proud, and grand, now irritable and wayward. Even the approach of death could not purge his soul of its evil humours, and he left a legacy to Cantillon as a reward for attempting to assassinate the Duke of Wellington.

*   *   *   *   *

But a reconciliation of his inconsistencies is not to be attempted. As the mood seized him he could be brutal, cynical, obscurantist; and who can keep the chart of his moods and thoughts? There is not a noble sentiment which he will not pitch overboard when the scowling storm is on him; there is hardly a proposition which stands unrefuted in the confused effulgence of his contradictory apologies. At one moment he loudly proclaims his beneficence, and then suddenly the notes of the edifying anthem are stopped, and we hear the chagrined cry of the baffled schemer laying the blame of failure on his confederates. On the whole he bore his hour of trial with a certain noble courage, cheering his despondent and irritable companions, and himself setting an example of resolute work. But, as hope after hope went out and disease gained on his constitution, his giant energy flagged. At the opening of 1821 it was clear that he had not long to live; and after the end of March he scarcely rose save to change his bed. The disease which slew him was the same which had slain his father, cancer in the stomach; but he bore the pain with patient fortitude and full knowledge. When Bertrand asked him what conduct his friends should pursue and what end they should aim at, he answered with fine magnanimity, "The interests of France and the glory of the Fatherland. I can see no other end." The last faint sounds caught from his lips as he expired on May 5, 1821, are said to have been, "*France, armée, tête d'armée, Joséphine*"; and so in the midst of the great hurricane he passed out of life, charging at the head of his ghostly legions.

THE ASSASSINATION OF ABRAHAM LINCOLN

(From volume VII, chapter XVI, " The Civil War,"
by John G. Nicolay)

From his parting visit to General Grant at Petersburg on April 3, 1865, President Lincoln returned to City Point, where he learned that Richmond had fallen and had been occupied by Unionist troops ; and on the following day, April 4, Admiral Porter arranged a visit to the Confederate capital for the President, the Admiral and several army officers. Proceeding by boat up the James river, the party started with ample conveniences for the trip. But when, on nearing Richmond, they came to a row of piles which had been placed across the river as a military obstruction, they found the opening through it so far closed by a disabled vessel that their steamer could not pass. With more zeal than prudence, the Admiral urged that they should leave behind their steamer, with the carriage and cavalry escort, and proceed in the twelve-oared barge he had brought along ; and, seated in this, they were towed by a small tug-boat the remaining distance to one of the Richmond wharves. Procuring a guide from the coloured men loitering near their landing-place, and without knowing how far they had yet to go, Admiral Porter formed the party into a little procession of six sailors armed with carbines in front, and four in rear ; and between these, without other escort, President Lincoln and his four companions walked a distance of perhaps a mile and a half to the centre of Richmond. In that southern latitude it was already hot, and the march was tedious and fatiguing, over rough roads and through dusty streets. Probably never before, in the whole course of history, did the ruler of a great nation make so simple and unpretending an entry into a conquered capital. The party at length reached the headquarters of General Weitzel, the new Federal commander, in the house which Jefferson Davis had occupied as his official residence only 36 hours before. After this, of course, every comfort was provided for President Lincoln during the remainder of his stay, and in his visits to the scene of the conflagration which followed the evacuation of the city, and to various points which the war had rendered historic. From Richmond the President returned to City Point, whence he took steamer for Washington, called back by a severe accident that had happened to Secretary Seward.

For a week after his return, Lincoln and his Cabinet were fully occupied with important details of administration, particularly with the serious question of reconstruction, which the recent military successes so suddenly forced upon them. On the evening of April 11,

in response to a serenade, after thankfully expressing the national joy
at the prospect of speedy peace, the President dwelt at some length
upon the difficult problems by which the question was environed.
Neither he nor his listeners had any premonition that this was to be
the last public address he would ever make.

The subject of reconstruction was again discussed in the Cabinet
meeting held on Friday, April 14. Lincoln spoke hopefully of
being able to restore the machinery of civil government in the
Southern States without encountering too much objection from extreme
radicals on the one hand or obstinate conservatives on the other, and
without excessive friction between the conquering and the conquered
authorities; and an unusual feeling of gratitude and generosity pervaded his words. The Cabinet meeting was made doubly interesting
by the presence of General Grant, who had arrived that morning from
the field, bringing with him Captain Robert Lincoln, the President's
son. The day itself had a historic significance. It was the anniversary
of the fall of Fort Sumter; and a great celebration was then in progress
inside the battered walls of that fortress, in which General Robert
Anderson again raised the identical flag which his own hands had
hauled down four years before.

In Washington on that evening, the President and Mrs Lincoln,
accompanied by two young friends, went to Ford's Theatre to see the
comedy of *Our American Cousin.* At about ten o'clock, while the
President, seated in an arm-chair in the upper right-hand stage-box,
was deeply absorbed in the progress of the play, a young actor
named John Wilkes Booth, a fanatical Secessionist, having gained
entrance to the little corridor, noiselessly opened the box-door immediately behind Lincoln, and, holding a pistol in one hand, and a
knife in the other, put the pistol to the President's head and fired.
Major Rathbone, who was in the same box, sprang to seize the
murderer, but the latter dealt him a savage cut on the arm with
his knife, and, advancing through the box, placed his left hand on
the railing and leaped from its front to the stage below. A spur that
he wore caught in the folds of the American flag which draped the front
of the box, causing him to break the small bone of one leg in the fall.
Nevertheless, he raised himself to his full height and, brandishing his
knife as he turned to the audience, shouted the State motto of Virginia,
" *Sic semper tyrannis,*" and, hastening through the familiar passages to
the rear door of the theatre, mounted a saddle-horse waiting there and
galloped away.

The ball fired by the assassin had entered the back of the President's
head on the left side, and, passing through the brain, lodged just behind
the left eye. For an instant the audience was stupefied by the pistol-
shot and the assassin's dramatic exit; then followed clamour and confusion in the effort to render assistance and in the eagerness of pursuit.

The wounded President, breathing but unconscious, was borne to a house across the street. Before such a hurt the skill of the surgeons was unavailing; yet his strong vitality was slow to surrender life. The family and State dignitaries watched by his bedside through the night, and at twenty-two minutes past seven the next morning Abraham Lincoln breathed his last.

Vice-President Andrew Johnson was in Washington at the time, and at eleven o'clock Chief Justice Chase, in the presence of a few witnesses, administered to him the oath of the presidential office. This formal ceremony passed almost unnoticed amid the profound grief and gloom that President Lincoln's death spread through the nation. On the 19th, after a brief funeral service in the East Room, the body was borne with solemn official and military pomp to the rotunda of the Capitol, where it lay in state until the evening of the next day, and where thousands took a last look upon his face. Then began a great mourning pageant, in which the remains were borne amid impressive and reverent popular demonstrations through the great cities of the States of New York, Pennsylvania, Ohio, and Indiana, back to his home at Springfield, Illinois, over almost the same route by which he had come to the seat of government as President-elect in February, 1861. On May 4, 1865, the body was laid to rest in the cemetery of Oak Ridge, where an imposing monument has been erected over the grave.

The elaborate preparations to assassinate the President were the result of a conspiracy which Booth had arranged and had been carrying on for some weeks, though the final devices of the plot were contrived the same day. Nine persons were active in the conspiracy, with a number of others, some consciously, some unconsciously, playing minor parts. The plot contemplated the assassination of several other high government officials, upon only one of whom, however, an attack was made. Secretary of State Seward was confined to his bed by a fracture of the arm and jaw received in a fall from his carriage. Simultaneously with the tragedy at the theatre, one of the conspirators named Payne, a stalwart but brutal and simple-minded youth of twenty years, pretending to bring medicine for the Secretary, forced his way into Mr Seward's bedroom, in the second storey of his house, and despite the efforts of Seward's son, whom he beat down with the butt of a pistol which had missed fire, and of a soldier-nurse whom he brushed aside, fell upon the Secretary, inflicting three terrible wounds in his cheek and neck with a huge knife. With desperate energy the Secretary rolled himself to the floor between the bed and the wall, and, baffled in his attempt, the would-be murderer again forced his way downstairs to the street.

Notwithstanding the weakness and pain of his broken leg, the assassin Booth, favoured by accidents, managed to escape first into

Maryland and then into Virginia, where, after almost intolerable exposure and suffering, he was, on April 25, traced to his hiding-place in a barn and shot, while it was being burned to drive him out. Payne was arrested on his return to the city, after having for two days hidden himself in the woods east of Washington. The other conspirators were soon ferreted out and taken into custody. After a long and searching trial by a military commission, during the months of May and June, four of the accessories were sentenced and hanged, three imprisoned for life at the Tortugas, another was sentenced to six years in jail, and the ninth, after two years of wandering about Europe, was finally freed by a disagreement of the jury.

The assassination of Abraham Lincoln caused a profound sensation throughout the civilised world. The deliberate malice of the murderer as shown in his preparations, the savage boldness of his deed in the midst of a great assemblage, the contrast of the black crime with the surrounding scene of brightness and pleasure, shocked every human soul not distorted by fanatical hatred. The sincere condolences and tributes of respect to the memory of the dead President that were sent by rulers and cabinets, by cities and associations, by individuals eminent in state and church, in science and art, came from all nations, in almost every language. These messages of sympathy were inspired more by affection than horror, for in the loss of this lowliest-born of men, whose genius had lifted him to the highest powers and prerogatives, who had shared the labours of the humblest and worn the honours of the proudest, all mankind felt a common bereavement.

He was beloved by his countrymen because he was the full embodiment of American life, American genius, American aspiration. No American statesman has equalled him in comprehending and interpreting the thought and will of the common people. He had realised the republican ideal that every American boy is a possible American President; and he gave the national birthright a new lustre, when, from the steps of the White House, he said to a regiment of volunteers: "I am a living witness that any one of your children may look to come here as my father's child has." It was by no means an idle forecast. Without even waiting for a generation to grow up, five American volunteer soldiers, who were under fire in the Civil War, have since then worthily filled the Executive Chair of the Republic. But it was not merely a romantic influence which Lincoln had on American life. He lifted the Declaration of Independence from a political theory to a national fact. He enforced the Constitution as the supreme law. It was under him that for the first time the American government attained full perfection in its twin ideals of union and liberty.

While foreigners could not so correctly understand or value his typical American characteristics, they were able to estimate his great-

ness and achievements for more universal reasons. At the beginning
of the Civil War, observers and critics in other lands, judging from
superficial indications, generally assumed that a permanent dissolution
of the Union was a foregone conclusion. Conservatives looked with a
degree of satisfaction upon what they deemed a certain failure of the
experiment of republican government. Liberals scarcely dared hope
that the Union would emerge from the struggle in undiminished
strength and territorial integrity. Both classes very naturally doubted
whether a rail-splitter candidate, even though he had the shrewdness
to carry a popular election, possessed the wisdom and the strength of
will to conquer a formidable rebellion. This question was now solved
by the test of experiment. Lincoln had reconciled, harmonised and
rewarded his rivals, crystallised the strength of the loyal States, inspired
financial confidence, dominated the jealousy of his generals, baffled the
intrigues of faction, and led the public opinion of his nation from
indefinite tolerance to the abrupt and total destruction of the institution
of slavery. All this he had accomplished with a sagacity, a tact, a
patience, a moderation, and yet with an unyielding firmness that made
his re-election to a second term at once a popular demand and a party
necessity. He had ruled with an intelligent purpose, a consistent determination, an abiding faith. He had administered a steady uniform
justice, and tempered it with mercy and forgiveness so ready and broad
that he was often censured for leniency and never for sternness. He
made liberal offers and grants of amnesty. Striking slavery its death-
blow with the hand of war, he tendered the South compensation with
the hand of friendship and peace. Commanding a million armed men,
his sole ambition was to vindicate the doctrine that the majority must
rule, that there can be no appeal from the ballot to the bullet.

To the admiration of foreigners for the art and magnanimity of the
ruler was joined their appreciation of his unselfish personal rectitude,
and his world-wide humanitarian wishes of freedom for the enslaved,
and hope for the oppressed in all lands. Above all, it was his great
act of Emancipation that raised his administration to the plane of a
grand historical landmark, and crowned his title of President with
that of Liberator.

CHAPTER IV.

THE CAMBRIDGE UNIVERSITY PRESS AND THE PRODUCTION OF THE HISTORY

AMBRIDGE was still a medieval town when John Siberch, the first University Printer, set up his press nearly four hundred years ago. The chapel of King's had just risen to the south of the old quadrangle but the buildings of no other college formed more than a single court. Twelve of the fifteen colleges then in existence stood in an irregular row, a few of them fronting, but more standing back from, some half a mile of cobbled High Street. Masking the front of most of the colleges, and here and there wedged between and around, were nests of red-tiled houses—students' hostels and townsmen's homes—facing either on the High Street or on adjoining lanes so narrow and so filthy that the most important of them was familiarly known, even in those days, as Foul Street.

Prominent in the town were the great friaries of the four mendicant orders. The Franciscans, whose buildings were perhaps the most splendid in Cambridge, occupied the ground where Sidney Sussex now stands. The house of the Dominicans stood where Emmanuel College has since risen, the Carmelites were between Queens' and King's, and the buildings and gardens of the Augustinian Friars covered some four acres close by the market place. Out at Barnwell, overshadowing even these foundations in wealth and importance, was the great priory of the Augustinian Canons. Across the river, where Magdalene is now, stood Buckingham College, a Benedictine house for student-monks, backed by the Norman fortress on Castle Hill.

The streets still swarmed with monks and friars in black or grey.   At night the proctors perambulated the town accompanied by priests and other ecclesiastics 'armed for the conservation of the peace' and ready to draw on laymen who disregarded their challenge.   Every few years came the plague.   The gloom of the solitude it bred on its last visit, six years before, had driven away Erasmus, Lady Margaret Reader in Divinity, the pioneer of new times soon to come.

In the High Street, in front of Gonville Hall, stood a house which bore the sign of the *King's Arms*.   Here Erasmus had once lodged and here, towards the close of the year 1520, his friend John Siberch set up a press.   Probably Siberch came to Cambridge from Cologne and his real name, as we should now regard it, seems to have been John Lair of Siegburg, a little town some twenty miles from that city. Little is known of the particular circumstances in which his Cambridge work was done, but the first book to come from his press, in February 1521, was an edition of an adulatory address to Cardinal Wolsey, delivered on behalf of the University on the occasion of the Legate's recent and ceremonious visit.   And while Siberch, for his second book, was setting Greek type for the first time in England, Luther's works were burned in the market place and the Cambridge protestants were meeting in secret at the White Horse Inn.

Nine of the books Siberch printed have come down to us in whole or part.   It may be interesting to mention that in some of these books he used the very initial letters which begin the chapters of this pamphlet.   His press has disappeared but a good idea of it may be obtained from the drawing facing the next page, which is reproduced from a

A Sixteenth Century Press

Book of Trades printed in the year 1568. And as this drawing shows a sixteenth century press at work, perhaps a few words of explanation may be given.

The men in the cut, then, by the leaded window at the back, are setting type from the *case* much as compositors do now in this twentieth century. In front, the printer to the right, next the head of the press, is shown in the act of inking the *forme*, or frame of composed type, with two *balls*, pads made of sheepskin, stuffed with wool or horsehair and fitted with wooden handles. Just a moment before, he has taken on one ball a little ink, previously worked up on a smooth stone; has worked it again between the two balls till both were evenly covered; and then has turned to his forme. The man by his side is removing a printed sheet from the *tympan*, a frame, holding a pad of blanket between stretched layers of parchment, which is hinged to the sliding carriage bearing the forme. When he has taken off his sheet we may imagine him replacing it with a fresh one. He would then shut down, over the clean sheet, the light open frame shown, to his right, resting against an upright support and hinged to the tympan on the other side.

This lighter frame, or *frisket* as it was called, when folded over the paper held it in position and kept the edges clean, for its openings only exposed that part of the sheet which would eventually come against the type. The frisket being down, the printer folds both tympan and frisket together over the forme. Then the carriage, now bearing forme, frisket, paper and the tympan with its pad, is run in under the screw press. The lever is pulled over and the screw descends and presses a stout board, called the *platen*, down on the tympan, and so forces the paper against the inked type. The pressure is released, the carriage brought out and opened and the printers are once more engaged as the cut portrays them.

Siberch at the *King's Arms* worked just such a press as this. Though the times were troubled, the printing-press under suspicion and the University authorities not usually over-bold, Siberch's employment as printer had no warrant but the enterprise of those he served.   But other counsels must have prevailed when, some twelve years later, letters patent of King Henry the Eighth formally gave to the University the right to elect 'three stationers or printers or sellers of books' to print and sell in Cambridge all manner of books approved by the Chancellor or his vice-regent and three doctors.   Under this grant printers were regularly appointed, but down to the days of Queen Elisabeth no more printing was done at Cambridge.   For fifty years King Henry's grant was used rather for the exclusion of heresy than for the promotion of learning.

But the Press, extinguished for a time by one theological controversy, was, in part at least, to owe its revival to another. In mid-Elisabethan times the Puritan party in the University was strong and its members were still hopeful of effecting within the Church of England those changes which were afterwards embodied in their own separate organizations. Without a Press they could do little.   In London the Stationers' Company had inquisitorial powers and not only might, but habitually did, search the printing-houses for books held to be perilous to religion or the state.   It would be difficult, if not impossible, to find a London printer to venture the risk of Puritan work.   In Cambridge for some years past there had been talk of a revival of the University Press. The Puritans threw their weight into the scale and in 1582 Thomas Thomas, a man of Puritan sympathies himself, was appointed University Printer.   From the day of Thomas's appointment—six years before the Spanish Armada set sail— down to the present time, the office has been maintained, and its functions exercised, without a break.

Thomas, and his successors for many years, used a press like Siberch's, set up in the house where the printer lived. Though the site of many of these houses is known, of only one has a drawing come down and even that is confessed to be 'drawn rather too short at the North end.'   But, however badly drawn, the sketch has a special interest, for the place was once the refectory of the Augustinian Friars.   So perhaps we may show the house, 'compleat, only made into 3 Stories,' in which Mr Buck, University Printer, lived and worked in the days of King Charles the First—with the defective 'North end' to the reader's left.

There was much to disturb the quiet of these early printing-houses. Bitter controversy raged for years between the University on the one hand and the Stationers' Company, aided by the Archbishop of Canterbury and the Bishop of London, on the other, and the University Printers bore a full share of the blows. So far as it concerned the ecclesiastical authorities the dispute was clear enough. The very reason that had made the Cambridge Puritans join in the revival of the University Press, led the Archbishop to dread it: 'ever sens I hard that they had a printer at Chambridg I did greatlie fear this and such like inconveniences wold followe,' he wrote on the appearance of a book in the Presbyterian interest, asking, in some desperation, 'for if restrante be made here and libertie graunted there, what good can be done?' With the Stationers the matter was not so simple. During the abeyance of the Press, the Company and certain of its members had obtained royal grants which gave them the exclusive right to print particular books. So, when they afterwards appealed to the Courts, their argument was that if the general privilege of the University to approve the printing of all manner of books were upheld, the University might approve, and, therefore, the University Printer might produce, books which the Company or its members alone had, by special grant, the exclusive right to print. But, when complaining to the Bishops, the stress, naturally enough, was laid on the moral danger of a press 'farre from ordinarie research'; 'it maie be thought we speake this for oure pryvate proffitte, but it is not soe.' In truth, though the Stationers had fair ground for dispute, in days when royal grants gave the only copyright, it is clear that their real objection was to competition of any kind from Cambridge. They did not want any revival of the University Press and they meant to prevent it if they could.

Thomas Thomas bore the first brunt of the fray. One day soon after his appointment he was busy on a theological treatise of the Regius Professor of Divinity. Doubtless the printing had been duly approved, for the writer, William Whitaker, was 'the pride and ornament of Cambridge.' Suddenly there appeared on the scene the agents of the Stationers' Company. They invaded Thomas's house, seized his press, his type, all the printed sheets on which they could lay hands, and carried off everything to London. Nor was the unhappy printer without insult added to his injury, for the Bishop of London wrote of him as a man 'utterlie ignoraunte in printinge.'

The University secured both the return of the captured press and the protection of its Chancellor, Lord Burleigh, for the ill-used printer, but the struggle which began that day lasted for seventy years. At times there was spirited action on either side. We have seen how boldly the Stationers opened battle. One of the University counter-strokes was to forbid Cambridge booksellers to sell or students to buy any book printed in London if an edition were even in contemplation at the University Press. Unless Elisabethan scholars were marvellously patient this order must have tried Cambridge men severely, and its issue shows the University as keen to defend the freedom of its Press as the Stationers were to restrict it. Success in the struggle passed backwards and forwards. At one time Star Chamber ordinances restricted the University to a single press, decreed that none of the printers should 'be suffered to have any moe apprentices then one at one tyme at the most,' and declared that no book should be printed unless it had first been approved by the Archbishop of Canterbury or the Bishop of London. At another time, Charles the First, then young on his throne, was persuaded to confirm the privileges of the University any letters patent whatsoever notwithstanding,' and the Lord Chief Justices, the Chief Baron and five puisnes upheld the plea that no patent for sole printing restrained the rights of the University Press.

Peace came with the Commonwealth, when Parliament, for good and all, recognized the University as a privileged printing place. And with the close of the struggle with the Stationers came the end of the domestic press which had obtained since Siberch's time. The change was made on the appointment as University Printer of John Field, 'printer to the parliament,' when the University itself secured a site for its Press, within a stone's throw of the present buildings. There Field built what was for those days a large printing-house. A colonist home from America who visited the place some five and thirty years later and 'had my cousin Hull and my name printed there,' tells us that the printing-room was sixty feet by twenty, held six presses and had 'paper windows and a pleasant garden.' The building, probably with different windows and a different garden, remained part of the printing office of the University for nearly two hundred years.

But changes of far greater importance were at hand. Field, a poor craftsman himself, was succeeded by John Hayes, and under Hayes 'great and excellent writinges' were sometimes 'much prejudiced by y͏e unskillfull handes of uncorrect printers.' Richard Bentley, scholar and critic, as yet in those librarian's lodgings at St James's where Newton and Wren and Locke and Evelyn used to meet, set himself to promote a second and a greater revival of the University Press. Then, in the time of King William the Third, were laid the real foundations of the Cambridge Press of to-day.

Many difficulties stood in the way. Hayes of the 'unskillfull handes' was Printer, his appointment was for life, and he was in possession of the only printing-house. The presses, too, were old, the type poor and worn, and the University without funds for their renovation. But more formidable still was the fact that no real control by the University then existed. Hitherto the Press had been the venture, not of the University, but of the Printer, who had taken gain or loss and made an agreed payment to the University in return for the privileges of his appointment. Bentley's ideal was very different. He looked to a Press which should worthily represent his University itself and should serve no end but the advancement of learning. His aim appealed to others, who freely gave him help, but, in the main, it was Bentley's energy that overcame the obstacles, as it had been his zeal that pointed the way. The first step was taken when the Chancellor of the University was persuaded to promote a subscription. When the amount fell short, the Senate was moved to borrow a further thousand pounds. Then a second printing-house was built, close by the old one, and there new presses were installed. Bentley himself procured beautiful type from Holland, very like some of the fine old-face type used at Cambridge now. And, finally, Curators chosen from the Heads of Colleges and the Senate were appointed to direct the new Press, with a competent craftsman, the Dutchman Cornelius Crownfield, as their adviser.

The noble Press, as Evelyn calls it in his diary, then established was, in principle, the Cambridge Press of to-day. Great as subsequent changes have been, Bentley's aim—the production of books held by the University itself to be of permanent value, in a way worthy of the work—has remained ever since the policy of the Press. In principle there has

The Pitt Building

CAMBRIDGE UNIVERSITY PRESS

been no change. But to some few of the vast improvements in method, affecting buildings, machinery and management alike, we may briefly refer.

First, as regards the Press buildings. When Hayes died the second printing-house was abandoned, and Crownfield, who was then made University Printer, was transferred with the new presses to the older house, which was the larger of the two. Some fifty years later, when George the Third had come to the throne, the first small part of the site on which the present buildings stand was obtained by the purchase of an inn which faced the old printing-house, across the street. Twenty years later, a warehouse was built where the inn had stood and, in another twenty years, this was converted into a new printing-house. The centre of gravity now shifted across the street and all subsequent growth has been on the side where the inn once stood. The great increase of work has made extensions almost incessant and it would be tedious to detail them, but just a word may be said of the buildings as they now stand.

The illustration opposite shows the front of the Press facing Trumpington Street, the High Street of Siberch's day. A share of the cost of erecting this block was borne by the surplus of a fund subscribed for the erection of the statue of William Pitt in Hanover Square, and the block is accordingly known as the Pitt Building. The main part of the Press buildings lies behind, forming three sides of a square of which the Pitt Building is the front. It may be of interest to add that the inn, which once faced Field's old printing-house, stood some fifty yards down the side street leading from the main road between the Pitt Building and the shops shown in the illustration; and that the site of the old printing-house itself, now occupied by the lodge and garden of the Master of St Catharine's, lies down the same street, on the opposite side of the way.

To turn to the improvements there have been in printing machines. For more than three hundred years from the arrival of the printing-press in England there was no great alteration in its make and no material change in its design. The new presses bought for Cornelius Crownfield must have been of much the same kind as the old press which Siberch worked. Some use of iron in their construction doubtless gave a lighter and less clumsy appearance, and the downward drive of the platen no longer rigidly conveyed the dead thrust of the screw, for a simple device gave some spring to the impression. But substantial improvement did not come till the end of the eighteenth century, when Charles Mahon, third Earl Stanhope, invented the press which bears his name. He used iron alone, which made his press more rigid, and, by an ingenious mechanism, obtained a higher pressure and a better stroke on the platen, so that he could increase its size and thus print a sheet twice as large as before. The first printing-house on the present site was built soon after this invention and two Stanhope presses were at once installed there. Another twenty years brought the first cylinder machine. In these presses—for now there are endless varieties—the forme remains flat but the inking is done mechanically by rollers and the flat platen is replaced by a cylinder which revolves, with the sheet, over the inked forme. Some account of the working of a modern press is attempted later, so it is sufficient to say here that the cylinder machine has immensely increased the speed at which it is possible to print well. The various presses of this general type which have been installed at Cambridge would make a long list, and the names might convey but little, but the principle of selection has been simple enough. Broadly speaking, it may be said that any new machine which could either improve the quality of the work or, without lowering the quality, increase the speed, has been adopted at the Cambridge Press.

Lastly, to glance just for a moment at changes in the government of the Press. Concentrated in a University there is a diversity of knowledge not to be drawn on, perhaps, quite so readily elsewhere. A University, too, enjoys an eternal youth which individuals can but envy. How best to take advantage of these special conditions in governing the Press, and how to combine learning, vigour and experience, was not determined without very considerable experiment. But some eighty years after Bentley's renovation there was evolved the present Syndicate of the Press, a permanent body whose members are constantly renewed, and from that time has dated the period of the Press's greatest prosperity. The Syndics, fourteen in number, are chosen from the Senate of the University, and included among them are some of the most eminent members of the various faculties, both literary and scientific. With the assistance of a Secretary and staff in Cambridge, and of their own publishing house in London, the Syndics of the Press carry on, on behalf of the University whose representatives they are, what has now become a great publishing business.

The production of the Syndics' books, with the other printing done at the University Press, is in the hands of John Siberch's successor, the University Printer of to-day. The Cambridge Press prints in every European language, in Greek, Latin and Hebrew, in Sanskrit, Persian and Arabic, in Hausa, Somali, Amharic and other African tongues, and in many other languages beside; its productions are known all over the world; and its work proves, if proof be necessary, that in printing as in all other crafts tradition and reputation count for much.

The Cambridge Modern History is a large work in many volumes. The numbers which have to be printed are great and have continuously increased as the successive volumes have appeared, and every sheet is printed at the University Press. Naturally many presses are used and these are not all identical, but, by way of contrast to the working of the old sixteenth century press, we may perhaps watch the progress to-day of one sheet of *The Cambridge Modern History*. Not to burden an account that must be but slight, we may imagine that the type has been set, the proofs read by the *readers* of the Press and corrected, revised and passed by writer and editors. Further, that every alteration made on the proof sheets has been carried out by the compositors, and that, from the type as finally corrected, *plates* have already been taken. These plates are simply mechanical reproductions, in metal, of each separate page of the set type. So the type can now be distributed and the plates, which take its place, are ready for the press.

The press on which they are to be put is a *perfector*—that is a press which prints both sides of the sheet in one operation. As it stands, a mass of metal some twenty feet long over all and weighing almost as many tons, with cylinders and rollers above, and levers, cranks and other connecting gear at the sides, it seems at first sight a crowded and complicated machine. But its working may readily be followed if, for the moment, we regard the press as made up of three main parts. The first, an iron foundation, consisting of two sides, some fourteen feet long and three feet high, and two ends, not quite so high and only seven feet across. The side pieces of this foundation are connected at intervals, at the same height as the top of the ends, by iron stays; and, above and at right angles with these stays, and resting also on the tops of the end pieces, are four iron rails which run the length of the foundation and project a little at both ends. So the foundation, as a whole, may be regarded as an iron table, without a solid top, but carrying four parallel tracks along and beyond its length. The second of our main parts forms a sliding top for this table. It consists of a flat iron carriage, nearly the breadth of the foundation and about as long, which slides backwards and forwards along the four rails, so that part of it projects alternately at either end of the foundation. And the third main part consists of two cylinders, nearly two and a half feet in diameter, which are fixed, side by side and almost touching one another, across the middle of the press, just above the sliding carriage.

At two of these three main parts we must now look more closely. The sliding carriage, we notice, has its upper surface, for some distance at either end, smooth and flat across its whole breadth. Between these smooth levels at the ends, are two sunken beds, to hold the type or the plates which replace it. These beds are separated from each other in the middle by an iron lath, which is set on edge from side to side across the centre of the carriage. Each of the beds occupies almost the full breadth of the carriage; the mere strips, at a higher level, which bound them at the sides, being called the *bearers*. The depth, from top of bearer to bottom of bed, is exactly the same as the height of a shilling set up on edge —for that convenient measure gives us the customary height of type. The smooth levels we noticed before, which bound the beds at their outer ends, are higher, though almost imperceptibly higher, than the top of the bearers. Now the plates we are to see used are mounted type-high; so that when two formes, each consisting of the plates required for printing a side of our sheet, are made up, one in either bed, the face, or printing surface, of each is on an exact level with the top of the bearers and only a shade below the smooth ends of the sliding carriage which carries them.

Now let us look more attentively at the pair of cylinders just above. As we have already seen, they are fixed, side by side and almost touching one another, across the middle of the press. When we watch them revolve, we shall see that they turn in opposite directions, each towards the other at the top; so that their inner surfaces, which come, half-way down, within an eighth of an inch of touching, are both always passing down towards the sliding carriage below. At first sight the cylinders may appear to revolve, each on a fixed axis, but on looking more closely we shall see that each cylinder in turn drops slightly, remains at the lower level for part of a revolution and then rises again. When the cylinder is down, its surface, at the lowest point, is on a level with the face of the forme. And the parts of the press are so connected and synchronised that the cylinder is down only while the forme which is towards the same end of the press is passing, on its outward journey, under the lower surface of the cylinder. At all other times the cylinder is raised, and when that is the case, the sliding carriage and its contents pass beneath it, without touching its surface.

We must just glance at the inking arrangements, which have not yet been noticed. If we stand facing either end of the press, we see before us, stretched across rather below the level of the sliding carriage and just beyond the limit of its slide, an ink-trough which is supported by projections from the foundation. The inner side of this trough is formed by part of the surface of a roller, which revolves and so coats its whole surface with ink. Against this roller, at the top, is a second roller which also revolves and takes ink from the first. This second roller is held at its two ends by pivoted arms, which, as the sliding carriage approaches the limit of its outward travel, rise and lift the roller upwards and inwards, so that it comes for a moment just on to the carriage as it reaches the end of its journey. Now we shall see the use of the smooth levels at the two ends of the carriage. They are ink-distributing tables. Our rising roller has deposited ink along a strip only at the end of the table. Were this ink taken up directly and rolled over the forme, the plates would be inked unevenly and in patches. So, as the carriage slides backwards and forwards, a second series of rollers, placed rather nearer in towards the middle of the press, work with a to-and-fro movement over the whole extent of the ink table, thus carrying the ink in from the edge and spreading it evenly over the surface. The transfer of the ink from table to forme is effected by other rollers, called *inkers*, which are placed quite close in by the cylinder. Each slide of the carriage brings the whole ink table under these inkers, except those few inches at the end which are the dumping-ground of the ink—for the carriage does not slide quite enough to bring that small outer strip so far in. So the inkers pick up well-spread ink only, which they then deposit, as the forme in turn passes beneath them, evenly over the face of the plates. For the difference we noticed before between the level of the ink-table and that of the face of the forme is so minute that the surface of the inkers can touch both, though the rollers press rather more heavily on the slightly higher ink-table than on the slightly lower forme.

It must not be taken that we have described, or even mentioned, every part of the press. To the mechanism which moves and exactly synchronises the working parts, we have barely referred, and there are many devices in the press, some of them essential, which have had to pass unobserved. Nor should it be assumed that names, where given, have always been used in their strict technical sense. Thus, for convenience of description, we have spoken of the whole part that slides as the *carriage*, though strictly that name applies only to the beds and bearers. But, in broad outline, we have attempted to display the main working parts of a modern perfecting press. Now let us watch a sheet pass through.

A pile of paper stands above one end of the press on a support which slopes gently down towards the centre of the machine and ends in an edge along the middle of the top of the nearest cylinder. Each sheet in turn is fed up so as to project just beyond the edge. This feeding may be done either by hand or by a special machine; but in either case the sheet, being ready by the edge, is seized by a series of *grippers*, or mechanical fingers, which come round on the revolving cylinder, across which they are set in a row from side to side. The sheet, held along its front edge, and so pulled, by these grippers, passes down on the cylinder. Now it will be remembered that the cylinder is raised, except while the forme itself is passing outwards below it. That arrangement prevents any soiling of the cylinder by contact with ink, for just as the head of the inked forme is about to pull out under the cylinder, which at that moment descends on it, the front edge of our paper comes round to the bottom on the surface of the cylinder. As the whole forme passes out, the whole sheet is printed on one side, between forme and cylinder, and the latter rises again once the forme has passed.

Let us keep our eyes on the sheet. As it revolves with

the cylinder and comes again to the top, it passes under the edge off which it was pulled, and it has now made one complete revolution. We shall see it turn on the same cylinder only for a quarter of a second revolution. For half-way down on its second descent, it comes, for the second time, to the place where the two cylinders practically touch. Now the second cylinder has grippers like the first, and as the front edge of our paper reaches the meeting place of the cylinders, both rows of grippers are adjacent. The grippers of the first cylinder open, the grippers of the second cylinder close, and the sheet is held, again by the front edge but now on the second cylinder, round which its motion continues. But what was the inner surface of the paper as it revolved with the first cylinder, has now become the outer surface on the second cylinder, and is ready for the second forme to print.

A quarter of a revolution on the second cylinder and the front edge of the sheet reaches the bottom. The slide of the carriage in the direction in which it was travelling while the first side of the paper was printed, has now ceased, the return journey has begun, and the head of the second forme is about to pass out under the second cylinder. Down comes cylinder to forme, with the front edge of our paper in between; and, as the forme pulls out, the sheet is printed on its second side.

Now that our sheet is *perfect*, we have only to watch it out of the press. It leaves the second cylinder just before coming round to the top, having made, on that cylinder, not quite three quarters of a revolution. At the point of departure, a drum, called the *take-off drum*, revolves against the surface of the cylinder. This drum carries a third row of grippers. As before, the grippers which have the sheet open, those about to obtain it simultaneously close, and the front edge of the sheet is diverted round the drum. It is pulled away from the cylinder, round a small half circle, and then released. Parallel tapes, which pass continuously round the drum and run downhill to smaller wheels some four feet away, on the side furthest from the cylinder, now carry the sheet along.

So soon as the whole sheet is clear of the take-off drum, *flyers*—long wooden fingers, pivoted at the knuckle—rise between the tapes, waft the sheet through a semi-circular arc, and drop it on to the *take-off board*, which is fixed at the end of the press opposite that from which the sheet started. There the *joggers*, four small boards set on edge, shift slightly in and out and continually pat, and so keep trim, the four edges of a fast growing pile of printed sheets.

Had we not been following our sheet, we could have watched the cleansing of the second cylinder from traces of ink acquired by carrying round on its surface paper which had been printed on the inner side but a moment before. This cleansing is effected by two rollers, covered with plush and automatically kept moist with paraffin, which revolve against the cylinder and so clean its surface. We ought to have paused, too, just for a minute, while the front edge of our sheet was still being pulled away from the cylinder by the grippers of the take-off drum. While those grippers still held the head of the sheet, and while the tail was still coming round on the cylinder, the empty grippers of the cylinder itself reached the top. At that very moment both cylinders had made exactly two revolutions since our sheet started, the sliding carriage had made one movement backwards and forwards, and the next sheet was just starting on its journey. Yet three seconds only had passed since its predecessor was pulled from the same edge on to the first of the revolving cylinders.

Compare the speed of a machine such as we have tried to describe with that of John Siberch's old press. The page of *The Cambridge Modern History* is a big one, nine and a quarter inches by six and three-eighths, but our modern perfector can take a sheet large enough to print thirty-two pages on either side. And it can turn out, at the rate of twelve hundred an hour, perfectly printed sheets, backed with that absolute accuracy of position on which a good result greatly depends. Each sheet having thirty-two pages on either side, or sixty-four pages in all, we have a total of 76,800 printed pages for one hour's run of our machine.

Now at what rate could Siberch work his press? He could only use a sheet large enough to print four pages of the *History* on a side. In one operation, he could print his sheet on one side only. And, work as hard as he might and with all proper assistance, he could not possibly turn out more than two hundred unbacked sheets in an hour. Those sheets would give him 800 pages for his hour's run—just the odd hundreds of our total of 76,800. Let us put it in another way. Work which would have occupied Siberch's printing-press for a full year, could be done, and better done, in about half a week on either of the presses partly shown, to right and left, in the foreground of the illustration opposite.

Printed sheets, however, are not the whole book, for there is still the binding to be done. The four bindings of *The Cambridge Modern History* are described on pages 104–5. As the work is not performed at the Cambridge Press but in London, and by various binders, it must suffice to touch here on two general matters, the understanding of which is essential to a proper knowledge of the bindings in which sets of *The Cambridge Modern History* are now published.

Some readers, perhaps, may be surprised to hear that, with scarcely an exception, books published in England to-day are not *bound* at all, in the strict sense of that word, when they reach their hands. Technically, they are *cased*. The difference between a bound and a cased book will appear from a glance at part of each process of manufacture.

In binding a book, using the term in its proper sense, the printed sheets are first folded, collated and pressed. Then they are sewn together and the thread, in forming the stitches, is made to pass round a number of *cords* which are held stretched across the back. These cords are pieces of stout hemp and their number varies with the size and weight of the book—for convenience of description let us suppose there are five. So, when all the sheets are stitched together, five cords remain firmly sewn across the back, in parallel lines,

A Corner of the Large Machine Room

CAMBRIDGE UNIVERSITY PRESS

with equal, or nearly equal, spaces between. Each cord has its two ends hanging loose. Afterwards, though at a later stage, the binder takes the piece of millboard which is to form the stiffening of one side of the cover, lays it against the sheets in the exact position it will afterwards occupy, and marks at its back edge the position of the five loose ends of cord. The millboard is then taken away and pierced with two rows of holes, each pair on a level with one of the marks, but one hole about a quarter of an inch, and the other about three quarters of an inch, in from the edge of the board. The board for the other side having been similarly treated, both are laced on to the sheets. This is done by taking each loose end of cord in turn, passing it round outside the back edge of the mill-board, in through the first hole and out again through the second, where it is cut off and secured. On the foundation of the boards, thus laced to the very sheets, the cover is then built up piece by piece. When it is finished, therefore, the cover is part of the structure of the book.

In a cased book, this is not so. In casing, a less expensive operation than binding, the process is this. When the inside sheets of the book are ready for their cover, a piece of *mull*, a rough, light canvas, is cut nearly the height of the sheets and about twice the breadth of their back. This mull is then glued down the back of the sheets so that a strip projects on either side. The cover, or *case*, has meanwhile been made separately, and is now put on and fastened by glue to the projecting strips of mull. There are two methods of doing this. The usual way is to place the sheets in position in the cover and then to glue the strips down to the boards on either side ; where, as a rule, they can afterwards be noticed under the *end-papers*, or outside sheets of the book, which are pasted over them. But where the book is to have a leather back, or a cover entirely of leather, another method is usually followed. The projecting strips of mull are folded over, across the back of the sheets. The sheets are then placed in the cover, the strips being glued, not to the boards, but to the inside of the leather back. This manner of casing leaves no trace of the mull under the end-paper and has the real advantage of giving rather greater strength, provided that the leather used for the back be sound and strong.   But in no cased book is there any structural connection between cover and sheets, or the prospect of a life approaching that of a book which, in the real sense of the word, can be said to be bound. Indeed, cased books are defined, by writers on the binder's craft, as books temporarily bound ; and the definition is true whether the cover be of the stoutest leather or the frailest cloth.   For the lesser durability of a cased book arises from the defect, not of the external covering, but of the internal structure of the book.

The second matter to which some brief reference should be made, concerns the quality of the leather used in those two bindings of *The Cambridge Modern History* which are true *bindings* in the proper sense of the word ; namely, the *Three-Quarter* and the *Full Morocco* bindings described on page 105.

The best, as it is also the most costly, of the leathers used for covering books, is Morocco—that is, goat skin, tanned and dyed on the grain side.   The appearance and the durability of Morocco depend both on the selection of the skin and on the nature of the processes which it undergoes before use on a book.   As to appearance, nothing need be said here, for anyone who sees a volume of *The Cambridge Modern History* in either the Three-Quarter or the Full Morocco binding, is in a position to judge for himself.

With regard to the durability of the leather, of chief importance are certain of the processes through which the skin passes.   The first of these, *bating* or *puring* as it is called, is a process by which all but a very small amount of the natural grease is removed from the skin.   Should this be overdone, the fibre is destroyed and the skin must be thrown aside.   On the other hand, should it not be carried far enough, then, when the skin comes afterwards to be tanned into leather, dyed and finished, the grease still left will cause it to discolour.   This fact has led to the introduction of a supplemental process of extracting surplus grease, after tanning, by the use of benzine :—a process, highly injurious to the life of the leather, which is not employed with the Morocco used for *The Cambridge Modern History*. But if the first removal of grease has been skilfully done, the skin passes undamaged to the tanning.

Morocco may be tanned either with bark or with sumach, the leaf of a plant grown in many parts of the world but, for commercial purposes, principally in Sicily. For leather intended for book covering, sumach is by far the better tanning material. First and foremost, leather tanned with sumach has a much greater resistance than bark-tanned leather to the destructive action of light, heat, gas fumes and oxidising agents. In the second place, sumach tannage leaves the leather soft and pliable, and with a white surface, while bark makes it hard and gives it a brown shade. For book-binding purposes, both hardness and colour are defects ; indeed the latter makes it impossible, when dyeing, to obtain many of the shades that are desired.

Sumach, then, is the better tanning material for Morocco intended for book covers. But there are two ways of using it. In one, the easier process, the skins are merely immersed, loose, in the pits or tubs which hold the tanning liquor, an infusion of powdered sumach with water. The other, the older and the better way, is known as bottle tanning. By this method, one skin is placed against another, each with the grain side outwards, and the two are sewn together round the edges. Before the joining is complete, the space in between the skins is filled with concentrated sumach liquor and a certain amount of powdered sumach itself. Then the sewing is finished, so that the skins form a bottle from which the inside liquor cannot escape. This bottle is floated in a large tub, filled with sumach liquor, and allowed to stay there till, owing to the fermentation of the liquor inside the bottle, transfusion sets up through the skins, the tanning is carried right through and the skins are turned into sound and durable leather.

It is by the latter method, based on the old practice of the Moors, that the Morocco used for the two best bindings of *The Cambridge Modern History* is tanned.   Save to those with some expert knowledge, it is not easy at any time to form an opinion of the quality of a leather.   It is still more difficult when that leather is pasted down, as in a book, so that only one of its surfaces can be seen and its substance cannot be felt.   But skins of the actual Morocco used in the Three-Quarter and Full Morocco bindings of the *History* are kept at the Cambridge University Press Warehouse, in Fetter Lane, London, where they will gladly be shown to anyone who cares to call and inspect them.

CHAPTER V.

O far, this little book, if it has in any way achieved its aim, has conveyed some idea of the origin, authorship and production of *The Cambridge Modern History*. It only remains to explain the special terms on which the work can now be obtained.

The sale of the *History* has always been great, but the Syndics of the Cambridge University Press are of opinion, notwithstanding that fact, that a large number of readers and students would be glad of the opportunity of acquiring so important a work by small periodical payments. They have therefore made arrangements, through their publishing house in London, to supply the *History* for a limited time on the instalment principle.

Lest the use of the words *for a limited time* should in any way be misunderstood, it should be explained that publishing houses do not, as a rule, deal directly with the individual book buyer. To do so in this instance, special arrangements have had to be made, and it would be both inconvenient and unnecessary to continue those arrangements for longer time than is sufficient to give the opportunity, which it is desired that all should have, of acquiring the work by payments which are within the reach of nearly everyone. The offer now made must therefore be temporary.

Those who wish to take advantage of the opportunity should tear out of this book the order-form they will find on page 107. When they have filled it up, they may do one of two things:—either post it direct, accompanied by a remittance of half-a-crown, to H. Department, Cambridge University Press Warehouse, Fetter Lane, London, E.C.; or hand it, with the same sum, to any bookseller, to be forwarded by him without further trouble to the subscriber. Whichever course they adopt, the books will be despatched direct from the Cambridge University Press Warehouse to the subscriber, and all further payments will be made—not to the bookseller who forwards the order and deposit—but direct to the Cambridge University Press Warehouse in London. Exactly what those further payments will be is clearly stated on the order-form on page 107, and is repeated on the last printed page of the book, for reference when the order-form has been torn out.

The eight volumes of the *History* which are now ready—the particulars, it will be remembered, have already been given—will be despatched immediately, and no further payment will become due until thirty days after their receipt by the subscriber. The four remaining volumes of the *History*, the volume of Maps and the volume containing the full and detailed General Index and Genealogical and other Tables, will be despatched separately as each is published. If the subscriber's home be in London, its suburbs or environs, or in any provincial town where delivery is made by the railway company, all volumes will be delivered free of charge. In other districts within the United Kingdom they will be delivered carriage paid to any railway station.

Hitherto *The Cambridge Modern History* has been issued in one binding only. That binding is one of those obtainable on the terms now offered, but it has been thought desirable to add three new bindings of a more permanent character. The least expensive of these, the *Roxburghe* binding described below, has a leather back and is *cased* by the better of the two methods described on page 99. It forms therefore a somewhat stronger and more durable book than the original buckram binding. The second of the new bindings, the *Three-Quarter Morocco*, though necessarily more expensive, is a *binding* in the proper sense, as explained on pages 98–99. The boards are laced to the inside sheets, the leather back is drawn on and brought round a full two inches on to the sides. The corners of the book are also protected by leather for a length of more than three inches. As the leather used is the sumach bottle-tanned Morocco about which a word is said on pages 100–1, it is not too much to say that this binding, save for the small part of the sides which remains unprotected by leather, is as permanent as any binding can be. In the third, and best, of the new bindings, the *Full Morocco*, the sides are completely covered by the leather, which is of the same quality as that used for the Three-Quarter binding, though of a somewhat finer selection. It may appear almost unnecessary to add that the volumes in Full Morocco, like those in the Three-Quarter binding, are properly *bound* books.

To detail the four forms in which *The Cambridge Modern History* is now obtainable :—

1. Buckram binding. Bound (i.e. *cased*) in polished buckram, dark blue in colour, on bevelled boards. Lettered in gold on back. Gilt top.

2. Roxburghe binding. Quarter-bound (i.e. *cased*) in brown Persian sheepskin. With raised bands on back and lettering in gold. The leather brought round about one inch and a quarter on to brown cloth sides. Gilt top; silk head-band.

3. Three-Quarter Morocco binding. *Bound* in sumach bottle-tanned Morocco, of a pleasant shade of green. With raised bands on back, the panels between lightly decorated and lettered in gold. The leather brought round two inches on to green cloth sides, which have also large leather corners. Gilt top; silk head-band; Morris end-papers; broad silk book-mark.

4. Full Morocco binding. *Bound* in sumach bottle-tanned Morocco, rose-red in colour. With raised bands on back and lettering in gold. Gold roll inside covers, carried right round on leather joints. All edges gilt; silk head-band; Morris end-papers; broad silk book-mark.

The volumes in the Three-Quarter and Full Morocco bindings are really beautiful books. More or less technical descriptions, such as those just given, often fail to convey a clear idea of the actual look of the books described. But arrangements will be made for the display of specimen sets of *The Cambridge Modern History* in most of the chief towns of England, Scotland and Ireland. Meanwhile, those who live in London, or visit there, are invited to call at the Cambridge University Press Warehouse in Fetter Lane, where they can inspect the volumes.

A book-case, specially designed to hold a set of *The Cambridge Modern History*, is shown in the illustration opposite. The volumes which appear in the picture are bound in the Three-Quarter Morocco binding. The bookcase is of fumed oak. Its design can be seen from the illustration, it is well and strongly made, and its measurements are as follows :—height, three feet nine and a half inches ; breadth of top, one foot nine and a half inches ; of body, one foot three and a half inches. If desired, this bookcase may be bought with the *History* and on the same system, but it is not sold apart from the books.

Those who prefer to pay at once in full, may by doing so obtain the *History*, in any of the four bindings and with or without the book-case, at a slightly lower price. The order-form given on page 109 for their convenience, states the different cash prices, and these also are repeated for reference on the last printed page of the book.

Those who have already purchased the *History* in the original buckram binding, may, should they wish it, now have their volumes rebound, in any of the three new bindings, at the prices given on the last page of the book. Volumes to be rebound may either be forwarded, carriage paid, to H. Department, Cambridge University Press Warehouse, Fetter Lane, London, E.C., accompanied by the proper remittance, or they may be left at any bookseller's, and the charge there prepaid.

Bookcase designed for
THE CAMBRIDGE MODERN HISTORY

www.ingramcontent.com/pod-product-compliance
Ingram Content Group UK Ltd.
Pitfield, Milton Keynes, MK11 3LW, UK
UKHW042151280225
455719UK00001B/255